HIGH FIVE ENERGY

BACKED BY $200 BILLION IN EXITS & IPOS

HIGH FIVE ENERGY

A DIFFERENT KIND OF FOUNDER

JEFFREY CHERNICK
WITH ALIX GITTER

Post Hill
PRESS

A POST HILL PRESS BOOK
ISBN: 979-8-89565-206-0
ISBN (eBook): 979-8-89565-207-7

High Five Energy:
A Different Kind of Founder
© 2026 by Yellow Visor Ventures LLC
All Rights Reserved

Cover design by Conroy Accord

Post Hill
PRESS

Post Hill Press
New York • Nashville
posthillpress.com

Published in the United States of America
1 2 3 4 5 6 7 8 9 10

To Ayla and Kailo, you are my everything.
And to the future innovators who will
deliver the dream of a better tomorrow.

CONTENTS

PART 2

INTRODUCTION

High Five Energy: A mindset, a movement, a method for impact.

For the last twenty years, I've built companies and raised multimillions in venture capital. I scaled my first company without raising venture money—just grit, strategy, and a steep learning curve that enabled me to hone and cultivate the skills required to create something from nothing. My second company was the opposite—fully venture-funded from the start.

Along the way, I became aware of a kind of magic—an energy that oriented things in my favor—a frequency I now call "High Five Energy," named after the micro-moment where two people meet in perfect timing and alignment. At its core, High Five Energy is the contagious, electric momentum that fuels founders when they are fully in sync with their mission, their team, and the opportunities in front of them. It's a state of openness, creativity, and action. A force that propels entrepreneurs beyond fear, hesitation, and self-doubt.

When you're in this state, *things just click*. Doors open. The right people show up. Synchronicities accelerate. You move faster, with more clarity and confidence. That's High Five Energy. It's a flow state. And it's real.

I've identified thirty-three behavioral shifts—each its own entry point to access High Five Energy. These patterns of thought, action, and perception are designed to help you break through limiting assumptions, recalibrate your mindset, and take action on your terms. These aren't steps to follow in sequence or rules you have to master. A single shift, practiced with intention, can unlock High Five Energy.

Whether you're starting, scaling, or selling your company, or wanting to build your network, find mentors, and connect with people who seem out of reach, this is your playbook for entering the High Five Energy flow state. Even if you're starting from zero, feel behind your peers, or lack the credentials of those around you, let's break through those *perceived* barriers and create amazing things, starting now.

And it's not just my story. To broaden the book's perspective, I've interviewed eighteen incredible founders with diverse experiences: from billion-dollar successes like Dollar Shave Club, Priceline, and Natera to high-impact exits in the hundreds of millions, like HotelTonight and Telesign. These include visionaries behind global brands, a top investor with $750M in returns, and a founder whose business, despite achieving a billion-dollar valuation, was brought down by the fallout of COVID. Their journeys—spanning exits and IPOs, scaling to billions in revenue, and driving profound impact—illustrate just how universal and adaptable High Five Energy's entrepreneurial principles are.

It's humbling to share these pages with the founders and investors I interviewed. My own entrepreneurial stories can sometimes feel eclipsed by the shadow of these giants of industry.

But that's actually the value of having both perspectives side by side. These themes span the entrepreneurial landscape and are applicable to the person at the beginning of their startup, the person who is actively running a successful business, *and* the person who's about to experience a massive exit.

We are at odds with the planet. The future is predicated on the entrepreneurs who think of the big ideas that will move us forward into a sustainable and healthy future. Now, more than ever, looking at entrepreneurship through a more conscious lens is *essential*, not only to unlock broader successes but to create solutions that are farther-reaching and bring more people along for the ride.

Anyone can create something extraordinary no matter where they come from. I'm not just an entrepreneur; I'm a drummer and a DJ. I throw massive parties on the beach. I make meaningful and lasting friendships. I'm not a "suit," though I once was. I am just like you.

As you read this book and start to integrate the principles in each chapter, you'll begin to experience High Five Energy, and the world will open its doors to you.

Most people become comfortable waiting for their time to come, but "most people" doesn't have to be you.

PART
1

PART

1

JUST FUCKING DO IT

My dad died at the age of thirty-eight. Every moment I spend waiting is a moment I don't get back.

When I was three years old, I awoke to paramedics in my house, my mom sobbing, and general confusion and dismay. My dad, a man who had recently gotten a job as a lawyer after taking night classes for five years, had a sudden heart attack and died in his sleep. He'd been complaining of chest pain for a year but was overlooked by doctors.

The impact of losing someone so important at such a young age is huge and lasting. The profound understanding that life is short, that every day is a gift, is embedded in my DNA. That event is largely responsible for one of my guiding principles: just fucking do it.

The Cost of Waiting

Standing on the edge of a decision or waiting to make a change until it feels "perfect" won't move your life in any direction until you do it. Yes, there is risk of failure, but failure is *certain* when you do not take a risk.

Part of why I get things done is because I know, on a visceral level, that I do not have all the time in the world. Life could end at any moment, which shapes the human I am today and the decisions I'll make tomorrow. From the deep importance I place on maintaining connections with people I care about to the decision to quit my corporate job because it was not fulfilling, my actions are always informed by the idea that tomorrow is not a guarantee.

Rethinking the Status Quo

When did we agree to the idea that life should mean sitting in traffic on the way to a job that drains you? When did we start measuring success by GDP instead of human health and happiness? Somewhere along the way we've been conditioned into thinking that we don't have choices. But there is always another way, another road to take, another path to consider.

You rarely encounter people who regret trying something. More often than not, people are regretful about the risks they *didn't* take and the joys they forwent in favor of staying comfortable in what was familiar. On your deathbed, you do not want to have any regrets. You want to bask in the memories of those moments where you gave it your all. Because those are the best times in your life. The moments where you weren't sure if it was going to work out, but you knew in your heart that you were living.

Dare to Risk: A Real-World Example

The principle of "Just Fucking Do It" isn't about reckless action. It's about understanding that life's biggest opportunities often come with inherent risks. Few stories illustrate this better than Matt Rabinowitz's, co-founder of Natera, a leading company in cell-free DNA testing that disrupted the prenatal testing space, with a market cap of $25 Billion. His story is a master class in taking action—not waiting for conditions to be perfect but diving in to solve a problem that was deeply connected to his personal experience.

> In my formative years, when I was around five—seven, I had a very rare hip disease called Perthes. I was kind of like Forrest Gump in these metal splints, but mine were much bigger and prevented me from walking properly. I wore them for two and a half years. As you can imagine, kids would make fun of me. In primary school in South Africa, kids were running around me in a circle for about half an hour over recess. When I turned to face one of the kids, another one of them would run behind and hit me at the back of the head. I still can't believe that kids can be that mean. I often felt on the outside because while everyone was running, jumping, and playing, I was dealing with these splints.

That experience shaped my desire to never accept defeat. I wanted to become someone they could not diminish. So, I focused on academics and naturally, I became very competitive. Everyone thought that I'd be walking with a very severe limp for the rest of my life because the splints didn't work. Instead, I ended up having a risky operation that changed my life. I was very lucky. I immediately took to my new legs, sprinting and playing a lot of soccer, rugby, and tennis—bringing that determination and competitive nature to my newfound freedoms. My mindset to stand apart and prove my value, taking stubbornness to new heights, is informed by that experience.

That tenacity is a driving force in my life. It underlies everything that I care about. The vast majority of companies have to be stubborn. They need to iterate and work through things in order to get to where they want to go.

So, when it came to Natera's inception, I was consulting faculty at Stanford and managing my previous company, which could use digital television—rolling out across the US—to create a high-powered GPS system that worked indoors, where traditional GPS didn't.

At that time, my sister gave birth to a little boy at Brigham and Women's Hospital in Boston. Only at birth did we find out that the baby had Down syndrome. I spent six days flying across the country, trying to support my sister and brother-in-law, who were sleep-deprived in the hospital, trying to make the best decisions. The baby lived for six days before passing away due to complications.

It was brutal. I kept thinking about how we have all this incredible technology in our cell phones, spaceships, and laptops and yet, it hasn't made its way into diagnostics. A child can be born with Down syndrome, and nobody knows it based on prenatal testing at the time. That drove me to think about how we could solve this problem.

The science at the time utilized rudimentary methods to assess if the patient was at risk. Based on findings like the nuchal translucency at the back of the neck from an ultrasound, combined with three hormone levels, you would get a test statistic that was meaningful, but not as good as it needed to be. The main issue being you had a less than 5 percent positive predictive value meaning of twenty high-risk results, less than one was actually positive. So, people were getting tons of these invasive procedures to confirm the findings, which had risks of miscarriage.

I came from a good Jewish family of doctors, so there was a lot of medical debate in my background. But I didn't have a medical degree. To some extent, that turned out to be an advantage. Because of my training in signal processing, which we applied to high-throughput genetics, we intended to dig the signal out of the noise with advanced computational techniques—approaches you'd be much less likely to take if your training was biology and medicine. We used engineering concepts to tackle a field that hadn't seen this level of innovation in a while.

Entering genetics would require me to start from scratch. There was risk in leaving the realm where I'd gotten awards, accolades, and where I was reasonably established, to go into an entirely new space, full of stuff that I didn't know. But I was determined. I bought graduate-level genetics textbooks and spent months teaching myself the fundamentals. I also knew that I needed experts, so I began building a team of doctors, geneticists, and statisticians to complement my engineering background.

Our first product was actually for in vitro fertilization. We always knew we'd focus on women's health, oncology, and the plasma space, but we built this technology initially to address the single-cell problem—because there was a clear issue that needed solving. We started by building technology for single-cell testing and dilutions resembling single cells. The existing technology was rinky-dink but few doctors who relied on the results understood that. We sought to show them that the current methods yielded false results. To do that, we sent samples using single cells from known cell lines and showed that the results were inaccurate. Most doctors were really supportive of what we revealed, but it was just shocking that people were using these technologies and not thoroughly vetting them.

Within a few months of developing our technology, we began applying for NIH grants. We didn't get the first ones, but we tweaked and evolved, eventually receiving outstanding scores. I felt validated that we were learning what we needed to and making rapid progress.

We ended up getting a bunch of NIH grants, which is an incredibly valuable process for a company to go through. Figuring out why your idea is better, putting the data together and describing it at the level required to win over an NIH reviewer, refined and validated our thinking. That made it easier to eventually raise money. A lot of our key IP—patents that have been incredibly important and truly transformative in their fields—came from that initial work we did to secure NIH funding.

The rates of amniocentesis and invasive tests in general have dramatically come down because of our non-invasive prenatal testing. We've totally changed the management of pregnancies.

The motivation for this work came from the deepest, most personal place. My sister was the initial spur to get involved in the field, but about fourteen years ago, I lost a child, too, from a genetic condition. That experience was medievally awful. The cause was completely separate from what happened to my sister. There was no genetic susceptibility. They were just two events that struck in the same family. But it broke me. Tenacity and strength did not free me from that horror and depression. It was overwhelming. Eventually, the engineer in me took over, and I became determined to have something good come out of this experience, no matter what.

We used a sample from that pregnancy when submitting to the NIH. That intention and desire was something I could cling to in my swirling state. That is when I said to the early team, "We are going to solve prenatal testing."

No matter what challenges arose, I was determined to solve this problem so that no one else would have to experience what my sister, my family, and I went through. We built the highest volume of clinical genetic tests in history, changing the management of pregnancies all over the world. Today, Natera's tests have touched millions of lives, reducing unnecessary stress, invasive procedures, and heartbreak. In the cancer realm, for example, we're saving many lives because we can catch the recurrence of cancers a year before clinical symptoms. Natera also has the world's highest volume clinical genetic test in oncology.

Matt's story is inspiring, and it's a powerful example of High Five Energy in action, showcasing the entrepreneurial values that drive success. From overcoming childhood illness to pushing through the steep learning curve of a new field, his journey highlights that there will always be many reasons *not* to do something, but taking action is key to creating your vision. Despite no medical degree, he dove headfirst into genetics, proving that a fresh perspective can bring breakthroughs no one was expecting. That decision—to just fucking do it—plugged him directly into the entrepreneurial flow state. His journey with Natera serves as a valuable blueprint for the ideas behind "Just Fucking Do It." He took aligned action, learned as he went, and ultimately created something transformative.

Make It Real: Your "Just Fucking Do It" Challenge

Success isn't about waiting for perfect conditions—it's about making a move despite imperfection.

Key Takeaways

- Waiting is a gamble. You don't have unlimited time. The "perfect" moment will never come.
- Regret stems from inaction, not failure. People rarely regret what they tried. They regret what they didn't.
- Action is the antidote. Fear, uncertainty, and doubt lose their power once you take the first step.

Your Action Plan

- What is one thing you've been putting off because you're waiting for the "right time"?
- What is the worst that could happen if you take action today?
- What is one step—no matter how small—that you can take in the next twenty-four hours to move forward?

AI Prompt: "I've been putting off [insert your goal] because I'm waiting for the right time. Help me create a simple three-step plan to start today, including one bold action I can take in the next twenty-four hours."

Make a plan. Do it. No excuses. The adventure only begins after you take that first leap into the unknown.

EVERYBODY POOPS

The job I landed out of college was on the corporate cash management team at Lehman Brothers Investment Bank. I worked for a guy named Sandy, who is a better salesperson than anyone I have ever met, before or since. He was like Michael Douglas in the movie *Wall Street*, a normal guy in person, but a magician when he picked up the phone. Sandy trained me to cold-call the CFOs and treasurers of the largest companies in the world who have hundreds of millions of dollars of liquid cash on hand. I was a relatively inexperienced twenty-five-year-old seeking to manage the cash balances of Fortune 500 companies. It was a little intimidating.

One day, Sandy turned to me and said, "It's important to remember that everybody poops."

This is my interpretation, and I'm sure Sandy would agree: Everyone has fears, they have hopes, they have dreams, they have families and friends. They get nervous about the unknown and excited about new adventures. *Everyone is human.* When you take a step back, it is clear that on a fundamental level, we are all the same. Adopting this perspective allows us to calm insecurities and create bridges that lead to connection. No matter who someone is or what they do for a living, whether a head of state or the owner of a local mart, people have the same basic wants, needs, and fears that I have. Embodying this concept brings everyone up to the same level playing field and makes it easier to connect.

When I picked up the phone and called the chief financial officer of a steel company in South America (who was managing $500 million dollars cash), I considered that he probably has a family, he probably sits in traffic, and he probably had taken a shit that morning. So, it became natural to nurture and close the deal.

To build authentic relationships, it's important to approach life with this key lesson as a central theme. If you interact with the world knowing that everyone is equal—everyone is human—then barriers are lowered and you can bring your full self to the equation. The pressure we feel when reaching out to someone new is lessened.

Authenticity Is Key

Why is that so important? Because in order to have a normal conversation with somebody, it's imperative that you be yourself. When I am authentic, not clouded by a potentially false calculus of who I think the other person wants me to be, I am grounded and present. I show up as I am, and I don't change faces based on who I'm talking to. People can sense that. Trusting that I am an equal to the otherwise intimidating person I'm engaging with makes it easier for me to be myself. They can in turn resonate with who I am, and we meet on genuine grounds. This creates a landscape of mutual respect, ease of connection, and a strong foundation for a working relationship.

The largest account I ever closed was a $1 billion deal for Cablevision. It was a one-day transaction that generated a lot of money for the company. What was surprising was that it just didn't faze me. When you work in the stock market, you realize quickly that human beings have created the construct of money as one of many systems to move and generate wealth; so, I acknowledge my part in contributing to that fantasy. This world is a made-up place fueled by the imaginings of us and the people that came before us. Our realities are shaped by our beliefs, so I chose to perceive things in a way that supported my success.

Shifting Perspectives

Intimidation is a huge factor that keeps us from being ourselves. The same can be explored in the reverse. I never assume someone has less to offer just because they are less senior than I am, have less experience, or come from a different background. The same advice I give to people about knowing their own value applies to how they see others. Humans are a fascinating species, full of surprises and unexpected talents. It's important not to write someone off before giving them a chance.

All of this "poop" talk offers another way to illustrate that so much of our reality is relative to how we perceive it. Perception is key in creating the job we want, the life we desire, and the world we inhabit. To that end, why would you perceive your boss as being intrinsically more valuable than you are, when you can perceive her as being someone who also wants the same things you do? Respect, love, compassion, friendship, success, health, family...

When you view the world as a community of equally valued human beings, the path to success becomes transformed. That ladder that we're taught to climb transmutes and flattens into a road that we can walk along in stride. Doesn't that sound easier? And more fun.

The Universal Spirit of Entrepreneurship

The following story is from my interview with Jessica Jackley, an American entrepreneur best known for co-founding Kiva, the world's first peer-to-peer microlending platform that has facilitated nearly $3 billion in loans and reached millions of people around the world. Her story underscores the ideas in "Everybody Poops," with a specific look at the entrepreneurial spirit that connects us all—from major world players, shop owners down the street, to the most resourceful among us making something from nothing.

> Right after I graduated college, I moved to California and took a temp job at Stanford Graduate School of Business. Importantly, I worked in the Center for Social Innovation, where every day students, faculty, and other thought leaders were focused on using business skills and entrepreneurial thinking to solve social problems. One day in 2003, Dr. Muhammad Yunus came to campus

to speak about his Grameen Bank. This was three years before he would win the Nobel Peace Prize for his pioneering work in modern microfinance. I crashed his lecture, and it changed my life. I was deeply inspired by his story and this incredible description of microfinance, and in particular microlending—so much so that I ended up quitting my Stanford job and moved to East Africa to work with a nonprofit called Village Enterprise, which helps end extreme poverty in Africa by equipping entrepreneurs with training, funding, and mentorship. They're a small but outstanding organization, and the work they do is remarkable. I was very lucky to have gotten to work with them.

I lived for about four months in different villages, moving around every few days throughout Kenya, Uganda, and Tanzania. I interviewed entrepreneurs, who had received one hundred dollars to start or to grow their micro enterprises, and studied how standards of living had changed for the entrepreneurs and their families.

I learned a lot of things, but most notably, I heard stories unlike the ones I had encountered my entire life about socioeconomically disadvantaged individuals in Sub-Saharan Africa. Up until that point, most of what I'd known about poverty I had learned from well-intentioned nonprofits that focused on telling stories of only sadness, suffering, and desperation, which they did for the purpose of getting me—a potential donor—to feel bad enough to give.

But when I was actually on the ground in East Africa, I met human beings with multifaceted lives. Of course they had, just like everyone has, stories of struggle, but they also had stories of triumph. They had needs, but also a ton to offer. They lacked so much but also made more out of what they had than I'd thought possible.

I wanted to share a fuller story about each person I met and to offer to others a way to connect differently—not just as a would-be donor. I wanted to create a way for others to lend, not just give, and to cheer them on and support them as entrepreneurs, not charity cases.

This was way back before crowdfunding was a word people were using! But my co-founder Matt and I thought, "What if we present these more honest stories of our new friends, and instead of asking people for a donation, why couldn't somebody lend money instead? Would that be so hard?"

Now, it turns out it was hard. But we figured out how to launch a pilot round of loans in the spring of 2005 for seven entrepreneurs in Uganda who needed $300 to $500 each. We spammed our friends and family and said, "We think this is legal. Anyone have some extra cash?" and cobbled together lots of tiny bits of money from dozens of people and sent the money over to those entrepreneurs.

Over the next six months, the loans got repaid. And entrepreneurs shared beautiful stories of change in their lives, things they had done with that funding; it was wonderful. Though small, we thought the pilot round proved enough to launch.

We put another dozen entrepreneurs on the site, spammed more friends and family, and repeated this process. By the end of the first year, we had facilitated a total of $500,000 in loans; the next year it was $15 million, the next $40 million, the next $100 million. Kiva will hit $3 billion in loans soon.

I get asked a lot about the "best" story I've heard or at least a favorite one. It's an impossible question, but I do love the story of Patrick, for whom I named my book, *Clay Water Brick: Finding Inspiration from Entrepreneurs Who Do the Most with the Least*. Patrick was a brickmaker that I met very early on during my internship before Kiva existed. He fled the northern area of Uganda with his brother when they were teens after a rebel group attacked their village. They left with just the clothes on their back, nothing else. They resettled with some distant cousins, but he didn't want to be a burden on their family.

Every day he would hustle and figure out how to survive. One morning, this entrepreneur was sitting on the ground thinking about his day, digging in the dirt, and he realized there was clay in the earth on his family's land. So, he started to dig and form bricks with a stick and his bare hands, and then sold them, for just fractions of a penny each. Doing this every day for months, earning fractions of a penny for these bricks.

At some point, he saved enough to buy a wooden brick mold. Production and quality increased, so he could sell more and for more money. By the time I met him, he had built several buildings in and around the village and had hired his brother and a few others too. He made something out of nearly nothing, out of just the ground beneath his feet.

I saw that again and again and again. Resourcefulness, incredible work ethic, the will to figure out how to survive by creating value however you can. I saw so much incredible brilliance, story to story, entrepreneur to entrepreneur.

In the start-up world, we tend to over-glorify one type of success. There's the monomyth of a tech bro in a hoodie who starts a unicorn out of his garage. There's a lot we should question about our assumptions around what "successful" startups—their founders—look like. I have found more inspiration in entrepreneurs like those I met in East Africa, and throughout the majority of the world, than in a lot of startup stories where a well-resourced founder made stuff happen. The entrepreneurs who build incredible things even when they start with very little, those are the stories I love most.

Jessica's story is rich with entrepreneurial insights and lessons. It was a very High Five Energy move to crash classes and take advantage of office hours when she wasn't yet a student at Stanford, bypassing conventional enrollment. For Jessica, her experience in East Africa shifted the traditional narratives of poverty. Instead of seeing people as helpless victims in need of charity, she saw capable, hardworking entrepreneurs with the same ambitions, resourcefulness, and resilience as anyone she encountered back in business school. She saw equals and leveraged that understanding to create a groundbreaking business.

Make It Real: Your "Everybody Poops" Challenge

True connection happens when we drop the illusions of hierarchy and recognize our shared humanity.

Key Takeaways

- Everyone is Human—No matter their title or status, people have the same fears, desires, and daily struggles as you do.
- Authenticity Builds Connection—Being yourself is the fastest way to earn trust and respect.
- Perception Shapes Reality—The way you choose to see people, including yourself, determines how you navigate opportunities and relationships.

Your Action Plan

- Think of someone you've put on a pedestal.
- List five things you have in common with them. (Examples: Movies you like, hobbies you share, etc.)
- Reach out. Send an email, a message, or start a conversation with someone you've been hesitant to engage with.

AI Prompt: "I admire [insert name or role]. Help me list five things I might have in common with them, and write a casual message I could send to start a conversation."

For all AI prompts in this book, it's imperative to keep emails and messages in your own voice. People recognize AI-written content. Within your prompt, give clear instructions to ensure the message stays 90 percent in your natural tone.

Want to watch the full interview with Jessica Jackley?
Visit: www.jeffreychernick.com

SEE THE FUCKING GRASS

"People around you are not necessarily the best judges of whether or not your business idea is very good, if it's going to be successful, or whether you have what it takes. If you looked at me, you wouldn't have seen an entrepreneur that had the pedigree to go out and do what we ultimately did, but you figure it out. Trust your gut and just keep plowing through the naysayers because they're out there."

—Mike Dubin, founder of Dollar Shave Club ($1 billion exit)

I'm now three years into a job that I didn't love. Suits and a side part, every day—not my scene. That voice in my head was getting louder, "Don't just sit around and wait! Take action!" A future working at Lehman Brothers or even finance wasn't the right path for me. I knew there was something more meaningful; something that I would be excited to wake up in the morning and work toward. I started the process by beginning to ask around about job opportunities. Friends, friends of friends, any contact I could get my hands on in the industries I was interested in (like advertising and marketing).

The Naysayers and the Doubt

I was either going to start my own company or begin fresh in a new industry. Time after time, I heard the same five discouraging words, "The grass is always greener."

People describing their own careers would tell me that their job may sound a lot better than whatever I was doing in finance, but in reality, it wasn't. "It's tough to start a company." "You're making good money." "The grass is always greener."

It's true that we can idealize jobs or things we don't have personal experience with. That saying is well-known for a reason. In the end, however, my dissatisfaction with my career proved stronger than the warnings from my peers and mentors. I wasn't happy, so I chose out. Frustrated with everyone's nay saying, I wrote in my journal, "Let me see the fucking grass!" I was tired of hearing how misguided I was. Let me see the fucking grass and discover for myself if it wasn't better.

And I'm glad I did.

Be willing to risk and challenge the idea that fulfillment lies elsewhere, or by someone else's definition. Stand up to the push-back of others and find out for yourself…because, again, at the end of your life, you're never going to regret the risks you did take, but rather the ones you didn't.

Betting on Yourself: A Lesson from Jeff Hoffman

Which brings us to my interview with Jeff Hoffman, an accomplished entrepreneur, motivational speaker, and humanitarian. He's best known for being part of the founding team at Priceline. com (with a market cap of $170 billion), playing a pivotal role in its early success.

I'm a software engineer. That's my degree. When I graduated from college, I got a job at a big engineering firm writing code. I did that for a couple of years and honestly hated it. I would walk in and think, "Am I just gonna be in this cubicle for the next twenty years?"

One day, the big boss, a guy named Charles, the highest-ranking technical person at this big company, emails me. He messaged me through an internal program that we used, similar to how Slack is used today, and he writes, "Hey, Jeff, could you come see me?"

Charles was many, many levels—all the levels—above me. At first, I'm filled with anticipation, thinking, "Wow, I'm going to see Charles—the guy that everyone aspires to be, the highest technical rank you can achieve…" An accomplishment that took him two and a half decades to attain. Charles had been there twenty-six years. And when he called me to his corner office, which was on the same floor as my small cubicle stationed in a sea of cubicles, I got up and started thinking about how Charles started in one of these cubicles just like mine. Probably right around my age, twenty-something, and now he is the highest-ranking technical person twenty-six years later.

And for no reason other than "I'm *this* bored," I start counting the steps it takes to get from my cubicle to his office. The hilarious thing was it was twenty-six steps. When I walked into his office, I had this grin on my face, so he asked, "What are you smiling about?"

What I was smiling about was that I realized in twenty-six years, he has moved twenty-six steps. That's it. Holy shit. Is that my future?

I didn't tell him because I didn't want to offend him, saying instead that I was just remembering something. But that was the moment I knew that this life, in this cubicle, was not for me. I couldn't believe that in twenty-six years he had only moved twenty-six steps.

I got to get the hell out of there. I quit that corporate job. My life's goal growing up in the Arizona desert was to see the world. When I would tell my friends that, they'd say, "Dude, you just need to go get a job. You're broke. Your mom's broker. No one is going to pay you to go see the world."

My thought was, *You're right, there's no job that will hire me to travel, but what if I could create one?* So there I am, no job, no paycheck, no income, no backstop when we started working on the first startup...

Most relatable to my own story, Jeff rejected societal pressure and expectations to carve his own path. His choice to break away from a career that wasn't fulfilling mirrors my own. Taking that first step and deviating from the conventional path is often difficult, but by refusing to conform, Jeff demonstrates that fulfillment isn't about reaching some idealized endpoint, but about living in integrity with your inner vision.

Make It Real: Your "See the Fucking Grass" Challenge

Breaking away from what doesn't serve you starts with shifting your perspective.

Key Takeaways

- See the "grass" for yourself. Most people project their own fears onto you, so follow *your* gut.
- Trust that exploration is valuable—Even if the grass isn't greener, you'll never know until you see it.
- Betting on yourself is a risk, but staying in a situation that drains you is a much bigger one.

Your Action Plan:

- Identify the thing holding you back
  - What situation, job, relationship, or mindset is keeping you stuck?
  - What's the "grass" you've been told isn't actually greener?
- Write your own "Let Me See the Fucking Grass" statement: capture the frustration that makes you need to see what's out there.
- Take one bold step: Apply for that job. Call that person. Sign up for that class. Drop that thing that's draining you.

AI Prompt: "I feel stuck in [describe your situation]. Help me unpack what's holding me back, then write a rally cry, and give me three bold next steps I can take to explore new options."

BECOME THE SOLUTION

"You can't help but innovate when you're trying to solve
a problem, especially when you're doing it with fun,
interesting people. Through the very nature of the pursuit,
you stumble on things that create innovations."

—Eric Pulier

I had a one-hour subway commute from Avenue B and 3rd
Street to Lexington Ave and 53rd Street. The other, more expensive, option was a ten-minute taxi. Waking up in Alphabet City
every morning at 6:50, the only people on the streets that early
were Wall Street "suits" and late-night revelers getting back from
all-nighters. The suits would typically be getting into taxis by
themselves.

Idea to Inception

I said to myself, "Wouldn't it be cool if there was a way to share a taxi?" I called my childhood best friend, Evan, who had a background in coding. I asked if we could build a website that would match two people going to the same place at the same time. "You mean something like this?" He replied to my email with a rudimentary version of the website, built. It was on. For the next year, we worked nights and weekends.

Launch Day

On September 7, 2007, we launched. I recruited a team—what we'd now call brand ambassadors—through Craigslist and enlisted some of my college friends. Dressed in RideAmigos. com T-shirts, they hit subway stops across the city, handing out flyers and spreading the word. I called in sick from Lehman Brothers and spent the day riding the subway with a loud-speaker, hyping up the street teams.

That morning, something unexpected happened. New York City had a taxi strike—the only one in all my years living there. My mom texted, "Oh no, this is terrible timing!" But I quickly saw the potential saying, "Maybe it's great timing."

Challenges = Opportunities

With taxis scarce, people were organically sharing rides all over the city. Every newspaper covered the strike, with headlines about strangers splitting cabs. I spent the following day emailing reporters, saying, "Hey, if you're interested in this taxi-sharing phenomenon, check out the website we just launched."

For the next two weeks, RideAmigos was featured in nearly every major New York newspaper. I was on camera at ABC News and NBC News, promoting our product. The site saw a massive traffic surge as people started posting their commutes, looking for matches.

In parallel, New York City taxis had just started installing TV screens in the back seats, half of them running NBC, the other half ABC. Those screens were intended to service advertising, but there weren't any ads running yet. I called the 1-800 number and got through to the head of business development at NBC Taxi Screens. I pitched him: Why don't I run a blog on my site, "NBC vs. ABC—Which Screen Do You Like Better?" The guy loved it. In exchange for the data, he gave me full-screen banner ads on NYC taxi screens for two months.

That was at least $100,000 worth of free advertising. Our site traffic spiked again, and the effort fueled growth. I, of course, used RideAmigos myself. Through the platform, I matched with a woman named Abigail who lived on my block and worked in the same building as me at Lehman Brothers. We shared a taxi for six months. If nothing else, I had proven the concept—I had solved the problem I set out to fix.

Adios Lehman

So, in June 2008, I made the leap. I packed up my stuff in a cardboard box, just like in the movies, said my goodbyes, and walked out of Lehman Brothers grinning ear to ear. I had escaped. The grass was greener.

We were at the very beginning of what's now called the ride-sharing industry. Around the same time, the founder of Lyft had a company called Zimride, a carpooling platform on Facebook. I remember hopping on a call with them to discuss integrating our tiny user base. Back when we launched RideAmigos, the number one response to our idea was, *Who would ever share a taxi with a stranger?* Now, in 2025, Uber and Lyft have since changed the world. Nobody thinks twice about sharing a ride with a stranger.

When you're thinking about starting a company, think about what could enhance your life or elevate your experience of something. Use your own journey as a starting off point in your search for the next big idea.

Solving Problems Is a Lifestyle

Let's continue my interview with Jeff Hoffman where we explore how identifying and solving everyday problems can spark innovative solutions that not only improve lives but also create groundbreaking businesses.

I got sent home my first day at Yale because we couldn't pay for it. Despite all the scholarships I received and financial aid, my single mother, who had four kids and three jobs, couldn't cover the difference.

So, I started my first startup in the basement of Yale below the dorms. In what was essentially a dripping wet, dark little room, I started my own software company to fund my education. Every hour that I wasn't working on my academic responsibilities, I was in the basement doing contract programming for companies in the surrounding cities. I funded the rest of my education and graduated in four years.

That's how I approach entrepreneurship. I never thought in terms of starting a company. I never wanted to be an "entrepreneur." What I wanted was to solve problems. It's an important distinction.

You don't become an entrepreneur. You pick a problem to solve and then you build the entrepreneurial ecosystem, the company, around that effort.

The first problem I solved in the travel industry came about during a time when, having barely any money, I bought an airline ticket to go see a mentor. Back then, you had to check in with a human being at the counter in order to get your boarding pass. The line was almost an hour and a half long, and I missed my flight. When you change a flight, you pay a change fee, but when you miss it, they take the entire ticket because the airline isn't able to resell the seat. That's painful when you're broke. I was standing there thinking, "There has to be a way to check myself in, instead of standing in a line for a boarding pass."

I then wondered how many people in this hour-plus-long line are pissed off right now. That's the first question: Is this a big problem that a lot of people encounter? The second question: Is there a better way? Immediately I thought about how I don't have to go into the bank anymore because I can just use the ATM. So why do I have to go up to the airline counter? Why isn't there an

ATM-like machine for tickets? So, I felt pretty sure there was a better way to check in. The third question: Is there a value equation? Meaning, will enough people pay you more for the thing you're trying to do than it costs you to do it? If not, then you have a hobby.

That day in the airport, I went around asking people in line, "How long have you been in a line?" "An hour and ten minutes," they said. I followed up with, "You seem irritated." Many were worried they were going to miss their flights. So, I finally asked, "Just curious, if I could simply hand you your boarding pass, and you could have skipped this line, would you give me five bucks?" People were saying, "I'll give you ten dollars." "I'll give you fifteen dollars." "I'll give you twenty-five bucks!" While I eventually had to remind everyone to "chill" because I didn't have actual boarding passes, I also was stunned at the potential business that lay before me. Because it ain't going to cost me five dollars to print a boarding card. All the criteria were met.

In order for you to be able to get your boarding pass and check in through a kiosk, we had to access the foreign language back office of the airlines—a communications language called TPF that was invented by the banking industry—pull up your reservation, and then turn it into English. Once we built that technology, turning all this machine code into an interface that allowed layman access to reservations, we felt the next obvious step was to implement that technology to booking reservations in the first place.

If you could now talk to the airline system (or hotel system, it's the same language) to access your reservation, why couldn't we just show you the airline options and the flights in a simple graphical form, and enable you to book your own flights? That was *the* force behind Priceline.

A unique piece of the story is that Jay Walker, the founder of Priceline.com, already owned IP on a reverse auction idea. His patent was for auctioning off empty hotel rooms—"name your own price"—letting people make an offer. With that idea in hand, Jay reached out to me. He knew that me and my team had built this technology and were well-versed in the tech side of connecting to all these systems. He assembled a group of people and said, "Let's all get together and build this thing." I went to Connecticut at Jay's request to be part of that founding team.

The real challenge was marketing because the internet was brand new. Not only did people have to get comfortable booking their own travel, but they also had to trust a system that didn't involve speaking to a human. Convincing people to enter their credit card details, especially for nonrefundable purchases, was a huge hurdle.

The marketing team brilliantly crafted the ad campaign around a feeling and brand personality, leveraging the iconic Captain Kirk. We are a travel company and what does the Starship Enterprise do? It explores the universe. Who better than a renowned leader known for his travels to represent Priceline? It all just fit, especially with that signature touch of dry humor.

Priceline kept reaching out to Shatner, getting rejected, again and again. Eventually, they offered equity, making Priceline the first company to pioneer a celebrity-for-equity deal. When it took off, Shatner made a fortune then every Hollywood celebrity—everyone in general—wanted a stake in an internet company. Priceline rode the wave of the internet boom and took off extremely fast.

The attitude, the DNA part of entrepreneurship, is that I've never been afraid of rejection or failure. You have two choices: You can try and, yes, you might fail. Statistically, you probably will, as the odds are not with you, but they're not zero. Or you can spend the rest of your life, wondering, "Could that have been me?"

What strikes me most about Jeff is how he doesn't let what looks like "obstacles" stop him from creating what he envisions. Like my personal experience with wanting to share a ride, Jeff personally experienced the frustration of long check-in lines and missing a flight due to an inefficient system. Rather than accepting it as an inconvenience, he set out to fix a problem. Developing the technology to make checking-in to an airline self-service led to something even bigger: enabling online travel booking. When you endeavor to solve real problems that people care about, you enter into a world that offers massive opportunities to create something really fucking awesome.

Make It Real: Your "Become the Solution" Challenge

The best solutions come from personal experiences and the drive to make life better.

Key Takeaways

- Start with a problem. Identifying real-world problems and questioning the status quo can spark entrepreneurial ideas.
- Act on insights. Jeff immediately validated his idea by asking people in line if they would pay for a solution.
- Develop a problem-solving mentality. Rather than complain, ask, "What could be a better way?"

Your Action Plan

- Identify a Daily Pain Point—Look at your routine. What inefficiencies or annoyances do you notice?
- Validate the Problem—Ask others if they experience the same frustration and if they'd pay for a fix.
- Research Potential Solutions—Investigate existing solutions and how yours could be better.
- Build a Simple MVP—Create a basic version and test it quickly with real users.

AI Prompt: "I want to solve [insert problem]. What are three ways I could turn this into a business? What's missing in current solutions?"

EIGHTY/TWENTY

"Perfection is the enemy of progress—it can hold you back and lead to trouble. The key is to step out of the lab and learn how to ship, iterate, and evolve based on real-world feedback. Where most people screw up is by getting stuck in their offices, chasing perfection, without gathering the practical data they need to truly succeed."

—Fred Krueger (ten exits with $500 million in value)

A lot of people get caught up in trying to make things perfect. They focus on perfecting their emails, polishing presentations, and holding themselves back until they feel "ready."

I live by a golden rule: eighty/twenty.

In my version of eighty/twenty, I believe being ready means getting past the 80 percent mark and then taking action. The last 20 percent is in the perfection zone, which simply put, is extra credit. Not only do I not always have time for extra credit, but "perfect" is pretty hard to come by and most often stalls progress.

I live my life by this principle. If it's good enough, move on and keep pushing toward your end goal.

People Are Busy

In the early days of RideAmigos, I'd spend hours crafting the "perfect" email. We would project the computer screen to a giant television and nitpick every word. It was tedious and maddening...and begs the question: Does the slight difference in sentence structure really move the needle one way or the other?

As I became more seasoned, I realized something valuable: people are busy—*especially* those who are successful. They don't often spend valuable time dissecting emails or processing them word for word. They assimilate the general idea quickly and move on to the next thing.

As long as I convey my ideas clearly, and they are grammatically correct, the precise words or phrases don't vary the weight of the message. The clarity of the central concept is what matters most. It's the same thing with presentations, proposals, and pitch decks. The general concept has to land and get the point across, the rest is extra credit.

Time Kills Deals

If you have an opportunity to speak to somebody, don't wait weeks or even months until you're "perfect," or more precisely, *feel* perfect. Seize the moment. That person will likely move on to other things if you don't. People switch jobs and adjust their priorities... There's an entire world happening for that person other than your experience of each other, so make sure to connect when the opportunity presents itself.

The point I'm driving home is that striving for perfection can keep you in the preparation stage for a long time, perhaps too long to effectively achieve what you're after. Executing on the creation of your vision is a process in and of itself, and there will be many iterations along the way. You will perfect and tweak your ideas as you encounter more people, obstacles, and feedback.

Keep moving, the snowball will build.

Speed as a Competitive Edge

Sam Shank, a tech entrepreneur, investor, and advisor, is a strong believer in this principle. He is best known as the co-founder and CEO of HotelTonight, a mobile app designed for last-minute hotel bookings. Under his leadership, HotelTonight grew into a widely recognized platform and was eventually acquired by Airbnb in 2019 for $441 million.

> I was a serial entrepreneur in online travel, which is basically another word for "glutton for punishment." I was working on my second company, DealBase, which began with what we believed was a great idea, but it never achieved product-market fit. While we were profitable, we weren't growing. I felt stuck.
>
> For me, making a meaningful impact on the world meant building something big, great, and truly significant.

I wanted to create something people loved—something that transformed the way they traveled.

I started thinking about different ideas, writing many down on a whiteboard. I had an iPhone 1, and the App Store had just launched. While looking in the travel category, I noticed that the travel apps were horrible. And it wasn't just my opinion, everyone was giving them one- and two-star ratings.

I was seeing other companies emerge here and be promoted by Apple—like Uber. I recognized what entrepreneurs wait for: a platform shift, a new opportunity to disrupt an industry, a place to build brands. I was convinced that billion-dollar companies were going to be built in the App Store.

What would a great app look like? Essentially starting backwards, I continued to think about what an app offers you that a website cannot, and I thought about how an app is always with you. It's geolocated. You can book very quickly. That led to very last-minute bookings, even after the booking window for many online travel agencies had closed down.

At the time, while exploring emerging travel companies, I came across Airbnb in its very early days. Even then, it was impressive, showing significant traction in marketplace liquidity. Intrigued, I reached out to Brian [Chesky, one of the two original co-founders]. We met a few times, grabbed coffee, and eventually, I visited the legendary Rausch Street apartment where Airbnb was founded and hosted its first guest. About fifteen people were there, but the energy was electric. It was clear they were on a mission to change the world.

Returning to my work at DealBase, I couldn't shake the feeling that I wanted to be part of something as transformative as Airbnb. I looked at my whiteboard, where I had sketched out an idea for what would become HotelTonight and thought maybe this idea wasn't just a good product, but a great business. It could be something that could truly change the way people travel. From that point on, I couldn't stop thinking about HotelTonight. It was inevitable. All that was left was to make it happen.

Because it was travel related and we had investors in DealBase, we needed to incubate it within the existing company and then spin it out. With approval from investors, we decided to allocate half a million dollars in seed funding from DealBase to build it. If we could gain traction and secure external investment by the time that money ran out, we would move forward.

We had our CTO from DealBase come over and basically single-handedly create the first version of HotelTonight. Then Jared Simon joined as the chief operating officer and was a vital, central force in HotelTonight, playing a key role in shaping our relationship-driven approach with hotels.

We moved incredibly quickly for two reasons. First, we had to; we were operating on limited funds, and time is money. The second is that speed is my personal approach to competitive advantage within a startup.

You can move very quickly. There's no one or committees to convince, no existing legacy code to work around, no outdated processes to slow you down. The competitive advantage is speed. The faster you get something to market, the sooner you receive feedback, allowing you to refine and make adjustments.

From the first line of code to launching in the App Store, we built HotelTonight in just ten weeks. We were selling hotel rooms right away, though it started slow at first. Our speed to market was critical. Though it was a forcing function of the limited amount of capital that we had, it allowed us to learn, adapt, and gain traction.

It's a subjective call, in terms of when something is good enough to launch. My rule of thumb is if you're not nauseated by how bad the product is when you launch it, you've waited too long. When we launched HotelTonight, while I was proud of what we had done, I could see all the flaws, deficiencies, and all the things I wanted to fix in the product. On the other hand, it did a lot of things better than anybody else did in the world. It was by far the fastest way to book a hotel.

Another initial constraint-turned-opportunity was that because we were doing a booking window until two in the morning, which was necessary for an app called "HotelTonight" offering same day booking, we couldn't do integrations because all of the existing systems ended at midnight or before. We had to build an interface to hotels where they could directly load the inventory in the industry called an extranet.

Being so quick to market, the integration was a phone call. We would call the hotel every day and ask how many rooms they have to sell and what they wanted to sell them for. That was the minimum way of getting launched and it worked.

We built more capabilities over time, but that constraint created an opportunity for us. Once we had a direct connection with someone at the hotel, they could load not only the last-minute inventory, they could then make that inventory unique. They could give lower pricing. They trusted us to be able to sell, sometimes exclusively loading it to HotelTonight. Had we gone through integrations, when hotels loaded available rooms in the system, everyone would have gotten the same rooms at that same pricing.

Again, the most important strategy when starting a company is to get it launched as soon as possible. You're going to get signal; you're going to get information. You're going to find out if it works or not. It should feel incredibly uncomfortable, almost nauseating, to launch something that early. People either have perfectionism that prevents them from launching, or they're afraid of competitors taking their ideas..

During the idea phase of HotelTonight, when we were just thinking, *All right, do we do this? Do we go all in?* I heard through the grapevine that Hotwire was about to launch an app. I thought, *Of course they're going to do HotelTonight, that's the obvious idea.* We wouldn't be able to launch it before them, and ours wasn't going to work. All the reasons not to try started to flood my mind, and I almost talked myself out of doing it. But then I realized: I believe in myself. I believe in our execution. I believe in us being able to move faster than a larger company. *Let's go.*

I'm glad I did because Hotwire didn't launch an app for eighteen months after that. Moreover, it didn't have any of the HotelTonight functionality. It looked just like the Hotwire website in a poor-quality app. I'm glad I didn't get in my own head and talk myself out of it.

I think the trap with a lot of startups is you can think that everybody has your unique insight. But not only do they likely not, even if they did, larger existing companies wouldn't be able to execute quickly enough on it. There is great advantage to having a small team that knows what they're doing and that doesn't have to answer to anyone but the vision they are striving to achieve.

Sam's approach exemplifies the eighty/twenty mindset: he didn't wait until every feature or integration was perfect. Instead, he launched the app in just ten weeks, focusing on core functionality, while accepting that there were flaws to address down the line. He prioritized speed over perfection, which enabled him to quickly test the market, gather feedback, and adapt. This decision, though very uncomfortable at times, was critical to HotelTonight's success, as it allowed the company to outpace competitors, even benefiting from what looked like initial constraints. By embracing the eighty/twenty principle, Sam turned what could have been a slow, stalled process into a fast-moving opportunity, ultimately disrupting the travel industry and creating a widely successful business.

Make It Real: Your "Eighty/Twenty" Challenge

The eighty/twenty mindset is about knowing when to push forward and let go of perfection.

Key Takeaways

- Progress beats perfection. The last 20 percent is extra credit. Get to 80 percent, and ship.
- People are busy. Focus on clear communication, since the fluff doesn't move the needle.
- Time kills deals. Opportunities don't wait, act now, then refine and iterate as you gain new information.

The Eighty/Twenty Audit: Look at a current project, email, or task you've been refining. Ask yourself:

- Is it 80 percent ready?
- Would perfecting it actually change the outcome?
- What's the fastest way I can execute it, while still delivering value?
- What's stopping me from sending, launching, or moving forward today?

Your Action Plan

- Set a deadline.
- Hit send, launch, or take action before the deadline.
- Track how it feels and what results come from moving faster.

AI Prompt: "Give me a simpler version of this [email/pitch/deck] that's still clear and good enough to ship now."

BE IN THE MOMENT

For me, being in the moment means being present to what is *right now*. It comes to most of us in fleeting instances, usually accompanied by a deep breath—a moment when time stands still. Being present in the given moment not only fosters deeper connections with people, but it usually clears away the chatter in your mind and offers deeper access to yourself.

A Shift in Perspective

This concept became clearer to me after I quit Lehman Brothers and moved to California. Evan, my RideAmigos co-founder, had an extra bedroom in Santa Monica. So, when his college buddy Matthew had finished an internship with the Obama administration, he had a place to stay while passing through Los Angeles.

Matthew described how he was off to manifest a house on a hill in San Francisco where he could live—for free—while building an intentional community. "Manifest" and "intentional" were words I rarely heard up until that point. But, a few weeks later he gave me a call and told me to come visit his house on a hill.

When I found myself at the Abundant Resources Community (ARC) in a town called Montara, I had intended to only stay for the weekend. While carrying a log to the group that was terraforming the land behind the house, I stepped back onto some uneven ground and busted my ankle. Instead of returning home to work on RideAmigos, I stayed for an entire month, and I learned to meditate and sit in silence. I practiced Qigong and cooked meals with vegetables from our garden. Most impactful of all, I read a book called *A New Earth* by Eckhart Tolle. From this book, I learned a life-changing lesson:

The Past and Future Are Illusions

- The past is done. Over, complete, unchangeable. Whatever happened *had* to happen, for the sole reason that it *did* happen. Our memories of the past change over time, making them tainted and unreliable. So why waste energy dwelling on them?
- The future is unknowable. There are infinite variables, and no matter how hard we try, we'll never predict what will happen. Yet, many of us waste so much time attempting to control or prepare for a future that will most likely not exist in the way we think.
- The only thing that has 100 percent certainty to be true and is *accessible* is this moment, right now. And just like that, it's gone…but a new moment is here. And another.

The Many Faces of Presence

My dance with the concept of presence is one that has changed me, and I continue to explore deeper meanings as time goes on. Presence can calm me, frustrate me, elude me, inspire me... but it's a worthwhile pursuit, nonetheless. Many people find presence in exercise, yoga, stillness, or meditation practices.

Bringing your awareness to the present moment slows everything down and allows you to take advantage of what is— to seize opportunity. Try it right now: take a deep, clarifying breath and notice the little things that are true in your space. (Light from a nearby window, a sound not too far off, the temperature of the air on your skin...)

Presence shapes other aspects of business and relationships, as well.

Presence Is Power

Recalling my conversation with great leaders, they all had one thing in common: They each spoke to me as if I was the only person in the room. They weren't distracted; their focus made me feel seen and valued. That is a very powerful tool with applications across many aspects of life.

When you are interacting with people, give them your focused time and attention. Don't check your phone, don't look around—simply, be present. Whatever else is happening can wait. In the thirty or sixty minutes of that meeting, you are much more likely to create an impact, a connection, and a memorable and worthwhile experience if you are actively listening and being present.

That brings us to a story from my interview with Scott Dudelson, an entrepreneur, investor, and professional concert photographer. I met Scott at an LA Tech event hosted by M13 Ventures a few years back. There's no coincidence that on my way to the event, I was riding my bike, blasting Herbie Hancock's 1973 album *Head Hunters*, which I hadn't listened to in years. As fate would have it, Scott is a complete music head. As soon as I walked in, we naturally gravitated toward each other and quickly became fast friends. What I didn't know at the time—something I would find out later—was that he had built his company Prodege, which sold for over $1 billion.

That brings us to a story from my interview with Scott Dudelson, an entrepreneur, investor, and professional court photographer. I had a consulting company producing benefit concerts, while also writing for a lot of music magazines. I really liked it, and I made a lot of great contacts, but I never saw myself as a good writer and it took me a lot of time to write.

During the initial stages of getting my company off the ground, I had less and less time to do my journalistic efforts. But I still had a crazy passion for music and live concerts. Every time I went to a show, I would see the little barricaded area...where the photographers would take photos.

They were right in front of the stage, with the best seats in the house. They would simply go home, download their photos, edit them, and send them off for publication. Meanwhile, I would stay until the shows were over, then stay to complete interviews and write reviews—both of which take a lot of time.

So, around 2006/2007, I had an idea: *I'm going to become a photographer.* I hit up one of my editors who I wrote with for a long time, and I told him that I was an amazing photographer—which was not true. I'd never taken a picture outside of using a point and click in my life.

He said, "That's great. I'll get you an assignment for a festival." Serendipitously, Linkin Park happened to be playing there. It was one of the first bands that I ever photographed. That day I went out, and I bought a DSLR camera.

I went to this festival, and I got hooked. Because the thing about being at a concert, when you see live music, moments happen and then those moments pass. If you miss that moment, you miss that moment. There's no going back.

When you're in the photo pit and the camera's up against your eye and Chester Bennington or whoever's running around doing something, there's only a moment you have to capture it. If your mind goes elsewhere, you miss it, you miss the shot.

It was pretty powerful because I'd be immersed in building my company all day, every day. It was all consuming. Its failure or success was on mine and partner's shoulders. Which was exhausting and took its toll on my psyche.

But when I was in the photo pen taking pictures, I had to be present to the moment, to the music, and the world melted away. In those moments, my business didn't exist. My dramas didn't exist. The only thing that mattered was the band right in front of me and the great shot I was going to capture. After that first show, I felt it in my heart, this is one of the things I'm meant to do.

So throughout the run of my Prodege career, at least three nights a week, I would go out and I'd photograph concerts, becoming friends with a lot of music photographers and creating a new network.

None of those people knew I had a business. None of them knew I did anything but music photography. Because when I was doing that, nothing else mattered.

The decision to declare himself a photographer without any prior experience is a classic High Five Energy move. It challenges the idea that expertise requires years of formal training. But what I love most about this story is how it highlights the power of presence. Scott didn't just chase success; he immersed himself in something that brought him joy. In the photo pit, with a camera pressed against his eye, nothing else existed. The pressure of his business, the noise of daily life all faded away. That's what being in the moment is all about. Entrepreneurship isn't just about external achievements; it's one piece of a larger holistic experience. When you're engaged in something that truly fuels you, it doesn't just make life more enjoyable, it makes success more sustainable.

Make It Real: Your "Be in the Moment" Challenge

Key Takeaways

- Being in the moment fosters deeper connections and clears mental clutter.
- The past is unchangeable, and the future is unknowable; this moment is the only certainty.
- Undivided attention is a powerful tool for impact.

Your Action Plan: Active Listening Exercise

- Have a conversation with a friend, colleague, or family member.
- Remove distractions. Put your phone away, stop thinking about your response, and focus entirely on what the other person is saying.
- *Reflect* before responding. After they finish speaking, take three breaths to process before replying.

AI Prompt: "Guide me through a one-minute mindfulness exercise using all five senses—keep it casual, not cheesy."

When do you feel most present? Can you bring more of *that* into your life?

Want to watch the full interview with Scott Dudelson?
Visit: www.jeffreychernick.com

MEDITATION

Being in the moment is a valuable and rewarding experience, yet it's not always the easiest state to achieve. Having a meditation practice is a great way to cultivate the skills required to be a steady force in the wake of the ups and downs that come with pursuing your goals. It's also one of my quickest shortcuts to get back into High Five Energy flow. Many successful entrepreneurs have some kind of meditation practice or means to calm and center themselves as the weight of what they are working on gets increasingly demanding.

Anytime, Anywhere

Without meditation, I'm pretty certain I would go crazy. I have found that just a few minutes every day changes the way my mind works. When you're having a busy day and you feel like the world's going to collapse on top of you, you can *always* take a moment to meditate and tap into that space where everything slows down. It's a valuable tool that you can pull out anytime and anywhere.

The masses are finally taking notice as well. You can see the increased understanding of its value by the growing popularity of apps like Headspace and Calm.

The first book I read about meditation was called *How to Meditate,* by Kathleen McDonald. The basic premise is there is no "one way" to meditate. Traditionally we think of meditation as being a silent time while you sit cross-legged somewhere on a mountain top. But you can meditate anywhere, even while walking your dog, on a lunch break, or in your car.

Matt Rabinowitz, co-founder of Natera—whose story we explored in "Just Fucking Do It"—describes a dynamic exploration of meditation that helps him cope with the extremes of entrepreneurship.

We knew how important these problems were and how compelling our data looked, which kept the energy high. It wasn't just about solving one problem and feeling the stress. It was about continuing the effort, knowing that once we succeeded, we'd tackle even more challenging and impactful work.

That mindset kept us moving forward. So, in order to stay calm throughout the storm, it's important to have a plan and truly believe in it. By focusing on the long goal, it keeps things positive and helps you stay resilient.

But, the other key, and this is very personal to me, is I meditate. At the end of my PhD, I was encouraged by this very cool Indian woman named Seema Bangar—she was dating my best friend—who would constantly tell me, "You're always concentrating, but you always concentrate on the wrong thing. You've got to concentrate on the right thing. You need to meditate." She was a very dear friend, so she kept harassing me. Eventually I hit an inflection point: I had just come out of a relationship, and I just finished my PhD. I thought, "I'm going to go and meditate for thirteen days and just see what it's like."

It totally changed my life. You get to a place where, after meditating for nine hours a day, on day six or seven there's just pain and rage and everything you can imagine in between. My instinct was to fight; fight the pain. But you can't because the more you fight it, the more incredible the pain becomes.

So, you get access to this place where the only option left is to step outside of yourself to see the pain and not identify with it. Besides the pain, you see all of what clouds your psyche: what people are saying or thinking about you, what you want to achieve and haven't achieved…and you recognize that all that stuff is just dust in the cosmos. When you can look at it all from that removed place, where you are not in it, and just be equanimous with what you're observing in your chattering brain, that changes your life.

If I didn't have meditation, I don't know that I could have kept going through all the stress. And there were a lot of times when I was paralyzed by the uncertainty of the future, not knowing what the path was going to be. But trusting that there is a path allows you to separate yourself from your ego, separate yourself from all the bullshit, and treat life like a game. And I could do that, not perfectly, but enough to keep going.

In general, a lot of people are intimidated by the idea of disrupting what they are doing to face their inner thoughts and delve inside. But taking that time truly makes things better. In fact, the mere act of disrupting the chaos to simply sit in silence for a few minutes—even if you don't experience an immediate result during the process—can prove very valuable. It can also set the foundation for a deepening of your practice as you continue to explore.

I've been meditating for over fifteen years, and if I go in and close my eyes, and take just a few breaths, having a few moments of nothingness, of peace and quiet in my mind, that is success.

Make It Real: Your "Meditation" Challenge

Key Takeaways

- Meditation offers clarity—you can create a pathway to presence on the go, and the stress of life and what seems to be important can be put into a manageable context.
- Anytime, anywhere—meditation can take different forms. There's no *right* way, or place, to do it.

Your Action Plan

- Start small and set a regular time. Commit to meditating for just two to five minutes a day. Choose a specific time each day, use an app to support consistency.

- Use a simple technique. Focus on a single point of attention—your breath, a mantra, or bodily sensations. Or try a guided experience.
- Patience and persistence. Meditation isn't about perfection; it's about practice. Keep at it.

AI Prompt: "Create a short meditation for me based on this mood: [anxious, overwhelmed, energized, scattered, or another state of being]. I've only got [X] minutes."

My favorite use case is to replace the classic "cigarette break." When work gets too overwhelming, I go into a conference room, close the door, set a timer, and meditate. By the time I am done, I feel like a new man.

Next time you're overwhelmed, give it a shot.

REMEMBER WHO YOU ARE

"We don't leave this world with the money in our bank account, accolades, the trophies on our walls or the news articles. We leave the world with a set of experiences. Did I love enough? Did I get loved enough? Did I experience magic enough? The day we sold Scopely for billions of dollars was a fine day, but it doesn't uniquely stick out in my mind because the greatest things in life are not the greatest successes in life. We put so much emphasis into the results of ambition: selling your company, selling a million albums, becoming a rock star, winning gold at the Olympics, as the way to achieve happiness. Then you do these things, and you realize maybe that wasn't exactly the key to happiness. If everyone had the experience of selling a company for a billion dollars, they'd realize that most of the things that make them happy, they probably already have."

—Eytan Elbaz, co-founder Applied Semantics
($102 million exit) and Scopely ($5 billion exit)

The Pressure to Succeed

While learning how to meditate and becoming acquainted with conscious presence, I was really, really stressed out by work. RideAmigos had been working on a collaboration with BlackRock Investment Bank for over a year, on a new ride-share system.

In the days before Uber or Lyft, banks and law firms would order black town cars for their employees ranging anywhere in the tri-state area of New York, New Jersey, and Connecticut. This cost companies upwards of $150 to send each employee home, five days a week. Through BlackRock, we partnered with the largest ground travel reservation company in the US called Global Ground Automation, or GGA. RideAmigos was going to add a ridesharing feature onto the greater GGA platform, allowing any of its thousands of clients to turn it on.

How it worked: Once a GGA client turned the RideAmigos feature on, when a ride was requested by an employee, the system would search for similar reservations. If the reservations had a similar route and time, the rides would combine, and the costs would be split between both parties. RideAmigos would take 10 percent of the savings. This is very similar to what Uber Pool and Lyft Line were pre-covid, but for the desktop.

This was a massive deal for RideAmigos. The taxi-sharing platform had just launched a year earlier. I was only twenty-six years old, and I had meetings with BlackRock Investment Bank, Goldman Sachs, Bear Stearns, and Lehman Brothers, all of whom were interested in leveraging such a service. I even had a letter of intent from GGA brewing, in addition to venture capital funding contingent on the partnership going through. Needless to say, a deal like this would change my life forever.

When Everything Falls Apart

Unfortunately, the CEO of GGA started going dark on me. I would call and email him, and every time we connected (often because he picked up the phone unexpectedly), he'd reaffirm that everything was going according to plan. Things were "just moving slowly," and I believed him. As time went on, not only was it constantly on my mind, but I started dreaming about it. The GGA deal was beginning to consume my psyche and make me miserable.

Just three months after I quit Lehman Brothers, the entire financial market collapsed. Lehman Brothers and Bear Stearns went under.

Sharing black cars was no longer on the priority list of travel managers. Even though the GGA CEO never officially told me that things were not moving forward, I eventually let it go.

The amount of pressure that I put on myself to be successful was crushing. My mother had spent a fortune to send me to college, and then I quit my six-figure job at Lehman Brothers (no severance) to start a taxi-sharing website…

Looking back, it's timely that my explorations with meditation were happening at the same time. It gave me the opportunity to self-correct and learn a valuable lesson from the experience. While reading the book, *A New Earth*, and meditating along the cliffs of Montara, my understanding of "identity" began to shift. As Ekhart writes:

> One of the most basic mind structures through which the ego comes into existence is identification. The word "identification" is derived from the Latin word *idem*, meaning "same"

and *facere*, which means "to make." So when I
identify with something, I "make it the same."
The same as what? The same as I. I endow it
with a sense of self, and so it becomes part
of my 'identity.' One of the most basic levels
of identification is with things: My toy later
becomes my car, my house, my clothes, and so
on. I try to find myself in things but never quite
make it and end up losing myself in them. That
is the fate of the ego.

Business Is Business

My identity is separate from RideAmigos. Truly understanding
this helped mitigate my anxiety about the success or failure of
my company. Its wins or losses are not reflections of my inherent value as a human being. RideAmigos is something that I'm
working on, it is something that gives me purpose, but it's not
the measure of my value as an individual.

Before this revelation, I was doing what many people
often do: merging my self-identity with some external factor,
in this case, with work. If the company's future was in the air,
so was mine.

After I understood that I was separate from RideAmigos,
simply put: I was free. I was free from GGA, from RideAmigos,
and from the destructive pressures of startup life. I was free
because I remembered who I am and my inherent value as a
human. That freedom also allows you to pivot, to think creatively, and be agile in an environment that isn't always easy
to navigate.

The True Measure of Success

Whether it be a job that you're getting hired for or the company you're starting, your true measure of value is qualified by who you are and how you treat others. When you can embody that separation, the joy in *the ride* becomes self-evident. The challenges that emerge are engaging problems to solve in the entrepreneurial game. The things that truly matter are health and the people that you love.

Overcoming the Odds

The following story is from my interview with Eric Pulier. Founder of more than sixteen companies, Eric has raised over $1.5 billion across ventures spanning artificial intelligence, cloud computing, open source, digital media, and blockchain, with multiple IPOs, acquisitions, and exits. He also pioneered Smart NFTs, launching the first unique, programmable blockchain assets through Vatom in 2015. He then licensed the use of these concepts and technology to co-found BLOCKv in late 2017.

> I'm so glad you can't go back in time and do things differently, because I certainly would and it would undermine my whole life now, which I greatly enjoy.
>
> There were obstacles that seemed insurmountable at times, that through a little luck and perseverance ended up becoming valuable gifts that led to mental breakthroughs and life-changing perspectives.

The first was in the early two thousands when I became the poster child for the internet bubble bursting. A company I'd co-founded skyrocketed onto Nasdaq and then hit the bubble along with the sector. When Pets. com didn't work, suddenly the whole world thought the internet was a fad. I think I was one of the top twenty money losers in the United States. While that was happening, my marriage ended shockingly, and I was left with a one-, three-, five-, and seven-year-old. I had lost far more money than I had, and the bills were washing in like a tidal wave. While dealing with an insurmountable crushing piledriver of emotion, I had to figure out how to support these little, perfect beings running around; three of whom were not potty trained.

At night, I was working on figuring out the next idea. In the morning, around 4:00 AM I would jump in the ocean off the coast of Santa Monica and swim. It was pitch dark, you couldn't see an inch below. I somehow conjured a startup vision to life. Sometimes I would go in the parking lot and cry for a little and then return upstairs to try and put on a good face long enough to take a step forward.

Then, I'd run home and dive into single parent life: dealing with someone sick, someone who needs a sock at school, someone who needs this and that…. In the midst of that relentless chaos and terror, at some point, I switched my mindset. Rather than spend valuable energy feeling frenzied or sorry for myself—and in moments entertaining thoughts that I was worth more to my family dead than alive—I explored what would happen if I could put that same energy into joy, play, and humor.

Things like Burning Man—projects that offer no inherent value other than to bring people together and experience communal creativity. I soon learned that creativity and love are really the antidotes to almost everything. They certainly were for me. And I shifted.

I can't say it was easy or all at once, but when I shifted around the spirit of play and the spirit of creativity it allowed me to become authentically optimistic again, to listen again, and to build again.

The second obstacle was equally dramatic, perhaps more so. In 2014, I sold three companies I had started on the back of a napkin. One was Desktone, a virtual desktop platform that became the foundation for VMware Horizon DaaS. Another was Akana, an enterprise API management leader used by Fortune 500 companies, later acquired by Rogue Wave Software. The third was ServiceMesh, a hybrid cloud governance platform adopted by some of the world's largest corporations, acquired by CSC. I sold it to this quasi-governmental organization, and I could instantly tell that it wasn't a good choice for me for a lot of reasons.

As I looked ahead at my future goals, I started to invest personally into several projects, including a vision for self-sovereign identity that drew quite a few colleagues with specialized skills into the project.

One day, I distinctly remember this moment, I was driving up north with my girlfriend at the time, and I got a call from the CIO of a major UK bank, and he said, "Hey, how are you doing?"

I said, "Fine. Sounds a little late for you. Why are you calling me in the middle of the night?"

He said, "Well, these guys I was going to recruit apparently just got fired from their jobs in Australia... and I'm told it's because they're moonlighting on some projects that your foundation funded and didn't get proper permissions." I didn't think much of it at first, as it appeared on the surface to be an HR matter, but I called to find out more.

I was reassured it was an HR matter that would be cleared up shortly, and I continued my trip without thinking much of it. But as the months unfolded, it started to become a bigger and bigger controversy. The company that had acquired mine was doing a $26 billion merger, and the last thing they wanted was complexity to clear up. While they supported me at first, they soon went into distance and protection mode and sought to take advantage of the situation and outstanding payments. We got into a knock-down, drag-out fight, and they brought in the government, who decided to join in on the matter.

So I started to fight. I had to fight the DOJ, the SEC, the FBI, and everyone else they threw in there to intimidate. It quickly felt like the dispute shifted from just a business disagreement, to putting my very life in jeopardy.

The decision on whether to give in to the DOJ or not was an intense moment in time. To give in and cop to something I didn't do would mean having that stain on my record forever. I decided that I would *rather die.*

It took me to the brink of madness. Five years of fighting the government was not pretty. When they want to win, they typically win. In the end, I have to give my brother credit for trusting that we'd find a way if we stuck to the facts and never wavered. When you know you're right, it's just a matter of finding the way.

We were running algorithms to prove our points with millions of docs and emails. And I'm not very good at that, but my brother is. Even my lawyers were saying to consider compromising in order to put it behind us. But we just kept hacking away and one day I think I was in the shower, my brother called me to say, "I think we got something here." We scrambled to get the information to the legal team and then it was time to wait.

While my expensive lawyers were presenting our final Hail Mary, where I was to learn if the DOJ would stick to their position, I was driving downtown, and just as I was about to hear the result, I drove down into the parking garage and the signal dropped! No parking on A, on B, on C…down and down I drove until I finally found a spot. I raced back up to ground level, and as I'm riding the escalator, I see my brother at the top and he says, "They dropped everything in the interest of justice. All charges dropped, with prejudice forever. You're done."

I couldn't wait to tell my parents and kids that it was over. Before long, the SEC's related civil case settled with everything I demanded to ensure my reputation was restored, and I moved on. Not just back to life, but back to a *better* life—stronger in every area, including my working relationship with the government itself, which is now thriving and full of promise once again.

Not many people get to go to their own funeral. When you're in a dispute like that, you get to see who runs, who stays, how people react. And in that process, you can't help but examine your identity.

Is my identity the things I do, or is it something more internal? I came to understand that my external reality becomes a reflection of my own mindset and internal reality. I didn't know that before. I still don't understand why that's true, but I'm clear that's how it works. That understanding helped reorganize my thoughts and how I want to spend my time, who I want to spend it with, and what I want to see in the world.

And you'd think that it would make me want to spend time more efficiently, but actually not so much. I want to spend it more purposefully. I feel much closer to my authentic self and more clear, joyful, and creative than ever before. While I wouldn't wish these experiences on anyone, I also wouldn't change a thing—I credit the journey for the destination.

Eric's journey reminds us that identity is not the summation of what you do or accomplish, but something deeper, rooted in who you are. He faced public scrutiny, personal upheaval, and institutional pressure. Yet through shifting his mindset and looking at the world through creativity, play, and sheer resilience, he reclaimed his power and redefined what success means to him. When the world demanded he compromise his truth, he stood firm. And in doing so, he discovered a deeper truth:

that your mindset—not your circumstances—shapes your reality. Eric's story is a testament to what becomes possible when you stop letting external forces define you and start building your reality from the inside out. Today, Eric continues to create future-shaping technologies, earning the trust of leaders across the world—proof that remembering who you are is your ultimate power.

Make It Real: Your "Remember Who You Are" Audit

Key Takeaways

- You are not your business. Your value does not come from your job title, the success of your company, or the recognition you receive.
- Your value is inherent. It comes from who you are and how you show up in the world.
- When you separate your identity from external achievements, you gain the freedom to enjoy the ride.

The Remember Who You Are Audit

This audit is a simple exercise that is meant to shed light on your relationship with your life and work. How deep you go is entirely up to you.

- What drives you? Write down the top reasons you started this journey.
- Where are you compromising? Identify any areas where you've been bending too much—whether in your work,

relationships, or mindset. Is it a necessary adaptation, or have you lost something essential?

- The Ten-Year Mirror: If you met your future self ten years from now, what would they remind you about who you really are? What advice might they offer you?
- The Reverse Bucket List: Instead of listing what you want to achieve, list what you would *never* want to compromise on. Does your current direction honor those non-negotiables?

AI Prompt: "I want to reconnect with who I really am. Create a workbook offering that asks me questions to reveal who I am. Something that can remind me of my values, strengths, and what actually matters."

Want to watch the full interview with Eric Pulier?
Visit: www.jeffreychernick.com

ALL IN

We launched RideAmigos as a taxi-sharing platform, but it was unfortunately "too early" given that mobile apps and GPS were not as prevalent as they would become years later. Plus, the GGA deal was long gone.

But that didn't mean we were done. Now based in California, RideAmigos started to take on projects to promote carpooling, specifically ridesharing, with government contracts. We started building event websites, survey tools, and various web services around what is today known as "commuter transportation." Essentially, RideAmigos was getting people to work with greener modes of transportation than driving, like carpools, vanpools, bikes, walking, buses, and trains.

A Big Opportunity (With One Little Problem)

One day, a large government agency announced a request for proposal (RFP) for a visionary transportation system. For context, RideAmigos was self-funded, and we did not have much cash in the bank. In fact, at that stage, Ben, our CTO, was the only employee getting paid. Evan and I were living off of our savings, and the rest went toward Ben's salary.

We decided to throw our hat in the ring. We had this idea to combine all of the tools we had ever created into one trip planner. Similar to Google Maps (on steroids), we called it an "Everything Planner." The tool would show all modes of transportation options and their relative environmental and economic impacts, such as the differences in CO_2 emissions, time savings, and money spent. Today, that is known as a multimodal trip planner. It had features for event ridesharing, gamification, incentive rewards, and even competitions between commuters. We pitched this conceptual combination and got to the final interview stage. The only problem was we needed to demo the platform, which we hadn't created. Yet.

The All-In Moment

We took the remainder of our money and resources and built the beginnings of that dream system.

Though incomplete, the site held together during the demo, and RideAmigos won its first major government contract worth $500,000 for the first year. That meant funding without having to give away equity.

We used that money to continue building the platform, which became the first version of the RideAmigos system. Today, RideAmigos is recognized as a trusted partner for ten Fortune 500 companies and thirty-nine major cities and states, facilitating smarter commuting for over five hundred thousand travelers across more than eleven thousand networks. With seamless integrations into over forty HR systems, parking hardware, and mobility providers, the platform has transformed transportation efficiency. RideAmigos's impact extends beyond convenience. By eliminating over ten million vehicle trips annually and reducing 175,000+ tons of CO_2 emissions, RideAmigos plays a significant role in global sustainability efforts. All of this was made possible because the three founders decided to put it all on the line in 2012 and build our vision of the future. The best part is that first government agency is our longest standing client and continues to take thousands of cars off the road every year with RideAmigos.

The following story is from my interview with Lynda Weinman, a computer instructor and author, who founded the online software training website, Lynda.com. Lynda.com was acquired by LinkedIn in April 2015 for $1.5 billion.

I had been a successful teacher. By this point, I had written a successful book. In the early days of the internet, my husband (Bruce Heavin) and I realized that with FedEx and the internet, we could live anywhere. So, we moved to a small town called Ojai, in Southern California, all the while still being asked to teach all over the world. My husband said one day, "Why couldn't you have people come to you instead of you going to them?" In many ways in our partnership, he was the strategist. That was a really big idea: Will people come to me? We rented a local high school computer lab over spring break when the school was closed, where we could teach computer graphics and computer skills. Additionally, we put an advertisement promoting the workshop on our website that had been publicized by the success of our book.

My book was so early that my publisher didn't have a website, and they put my personal URL on my book. This drove all this traffic to Lynda.com well before social media existed. Before you could "go viral," we went viral.

The workshop sold out, attracting people from all over the world. Someone even came from Vienna, Austria, to our first class at a local high school in our tiny little town. This led to my husband having another big idea: "Let's rent our own space, create our own computer lab, which we can use as our own studio when we're not doing classes and offer classes whenever we want."

That initial success with our first workshop gave us the courage to take our entire life savings, which was $20,000, buy computers, and rent a space. Within two or three months, we were in the black, and we had paid ourselves back.

In the beginning of Lynda.com, we were experiencing great success as a brick-and-mortar classroom. We had people coming from all over the country and all over the world to our classes. It was very early in the internet, and people were eager to capitalize and get rich by having a website. Tons of venture money was pouring into the space. And we were the only place pretty much on earth where you could learn comprehensive web design—it wasn't even taught in college yet. We were at the forefront of this new and emerging industry.

Then 9/11. When the attacks happened, the whole country shut down—similar to our more recent experience with COVID. It was an earth-shattering moment in history where everything changed, airline flights were grounded for a month. The events of 9/11 marked a turning point for our company, prompting the biggest pivot in our trajectory: deciding to put our lessons online. That shift turned out to be a far bigger idea than we could have imagined.

As we were transitioning everything from books and analog formats to digital delivery—shifting from one-to-one teaching to a one-to-many model, our competitors in software training were expanding through physical offices and classrooms and selling videotapes. We decided to make it a "lean back" experience, not "lean forward," and went all-in on our pivot to digital and our subscription model.

But in the beginning, it did not go well for us. It actually cannibalized our classes. The cost was only twenty-five dollars a month, a lot less than buying a video at $150, so it cannibalized our sales of VHS tapes, which don't even exist anymore, as well. Since we had already started making video classes, we continued down that path and launched our subscription service—very early days of the subscription service model.

We took a poll around the office—at the time, we had about twenty employees—to guess how many subscribers we would have in the first month. Nobody guessed low enough, because it was around twenty subscribers, far fewer than the team had anticipated. I even attended a subscription conference, probably around 2006 or 2007, where I heard someone say, "To build a successful subscription company, you must first walk through the desert." And that's exactly what we did.

Over the first year, we grew to about one thousand subscribers, which still felt underwhelming compared to expectations. Year two, we had two thousand subscribers. Year three, we had four thousand subscribers. My brilliant husband, once again, noted that this is actually growing incredibly fast, even though it felt like molasses to me. There were moments where I even talked about selling the video arm of our company because it was a "failure."

He wrote down on a piece of paper what, for all intents and purposes, was a spreadsheet with all these figures notes, all in his handwriting, projecting the value of what we were creating. Eight years later, I found that piece of paper, and he was almost right to the dollar of what we were going to be earning.

Before we started Lynda.com I had taught at ArtCenter for years and also taught evening classes at UCLA and the American Film Institute. I was a working schoolteacher, a gig worker, earning twenty-five to thirty dollars an hour. As a single mom, I supported myself, and I was proud of it. But my mom was always on my case, saying I never did anything with the family or went anywhere. She'd say I worked so hard and had nothing to show for it. But what I had to show for it was that I loved what I was doing, and I got paid for it. To me, that was a privilege.

We were offered investment before we were ready and turned it down. Bruce and I had a $70 million valuation and were offered $10 million for a stake in our company. We declined because we didn't need the money and didn't want to lose control of the company. We still had so much more to do, and we were so deeply invested in it. Your point about passion resonates—I'd have done what I loved, and did for many years, for far less.

Then came my unexpected, spectacular exit, which was never the goal. Investors came knocking because we had built a profitable business. We were not only making money, but also putting a great product into the world, helping people, and treating our employees well. It was the dream—we were living the dream.

Again, I was a teacher, he was not a teacher. It took the two of us in this dynamic but equal partnership, balancing different skills and strengths, to achieve what we accomplished.

Lynda's story epitomizes the value of going "All In" on your passions. First there was the literal "All In" moment when Lynda and her husband, Bruce, poured their life savings into the initial investment for their "brick and mortar" classroom and the computers they would need to teach class. Then *again* Linda went all in, risking their already successful business, to move online and pivot to a subscription model. She and Bruce had to trust the long-term strategy would pay off, and it was a good bet. The path before you may not always be clear, but if you have clarity of vision, of passion, and of purpose, you can navigate that uncertainty and make that important bet: going all in on *yourself.*

Make It Real: Your "All In" Challenge

There is no greater thrill than going for the gold.

Key Takeaways

- Bet on yourself and your vision.
- Timing isn't always in your control, but persistence is.
- Strike while the iron is hot. Opportunities don't wait for perfect conditions.

Your Action Plan

Think about a project, idea, or opportunity that excites you, but where you've been holding back.

- Identify the Leap: What's the boldest move you could make to push it forward?
- Find the Risk: What's stopping you? What's the worst-case scenario? How could you mitigate it?
- Commit to Action: What's one decision or step you can take right now to go all in?

AI Prompt: "I've been working on an opportunity in [insert area]. Help me define what 'going all in' would look like—practically, emotionally, and publicly. Is the juice worth the squeeze?"
LFG.

GIVE, GIVE, GET

"This vision's interest is about service. Serving our users, supporting our employees, and at the same time, prioritizing education and conservation to create a more just and accurate world. That's why we provide our software to twenty thousand schools, support twelve thousand universities, and invest in conservation efforts not just in California, but in Argentina, Uganda, and beyond. We can do these things, not instead of, not as a result of, but run them in parallel, achieving a more holistic life. Living a purposeful life, for me, is important."

—Jack Dangermond, co-founder of Esri
($2 billion in annual revenue)

A Simple Truth

The more you give, the more you get—a simple philosophy with the power to change everything. Some people call it karma; others call it the law of attraction. Whatever name you choose, the principle holds true: the more you put into the world, the more you will receive from it. It's a compelling concept that, at first, might seem abstract or idealistic, but the more I practice it, the more undeniable its truth becomes. Giving is not merely an act of charity; it is an investment in the fabric of humanity, a force that reverberates far beyond the initial gesture.

I completed an effective, six-month emotional intelligence program in Los Angeles. More than just a seminar, it was a full-spectrum immersion into personal development, self-awareness, and conscious leadership. It provided tools for strengthening my relationships and cultivating success, but also an unwavering call to action: *give, give, get.* The program created parameters for engaging with that philosophical model in my daily life.

Whether I was volunteering at a soup kitchen or giving out free hugs on the street, giving was like a drug, and the fulfillment I received in return kept me coming back for more. The more I gave of myself in service to others, the more the universe gave back to me in myriad and unexpected ways.

Unexpected ROI

In the throes of practicing this exercise, I was posting on Facebook, offering my time and advice to anyone who wanted to connect. The universe did indeed answer, but let's first back up a little.

Two years prior to that training, my band, an electro synth duo called Story of the Running Wolf, played at Lightning in a Bottle, an annual music, arts, and cultural festival held in California. After our show, a fan approached a man named Paul with our CD. Given that our album art was a cartoon version of my face, and Paul looked *very* much like me, it was no surprise when Paul was asked for my autograph. Not knowing the band and knowing he'd never see the guy again, Paul gladly played along and signed the record.

A year later, in complete coincidence through mutual friends, we camped together at the same festival. My band played again and when we met, he put two and two together.

"Oh my God!" Paul said. "You're the guy from the CD!" It was quite the unlikely coincidence, and it doesn't stop there.

One year after that realization, we are now caught back up to my training. Paul received a free ticket to LA Startup Weekend. Startup Weekend is an event where entrepreneurs, designers, and developers come together for one weekend to incubate startups. Entrepreneurs pitch their ideas, and participants vote the best ones into teams, and by the end of the weekend, they develop an MVP (minimum viable product). The teams present to judges from accelerators, venture funds, and the like for prizes.

Now here's where we circle back to my exercise with give, give, get. Paul asked his friend if he knew anyone with good ideas. Because I was actively sharing insights on entrepreneurship on Facebook—offering value with no expectations for returns—his friend saw my posts and reconnected Paul and me. "You should speak to Jeffrey Chernick, he's got ideas."

The Idea

At some point in my life, a friend had left a voice memo on my phone, and I assigned it to his ringtone. When he called me, I heard his voice. I thought to myself, "Wouldn't it be cool if I could set the ringtone on my friend's phone so they heard my voice when I called them?" This technology would essentially push a recorded ringtone to another device. I called it Ring-A-Ling. I had a PowerPoint investment presentation ready to go, but since I was busy with RideAmigos and didn't really know much about the mobile apps scene, I had been sitting on the idea for some time.

When Paul came to me asking for an idea to pitch at LA Startup Weekend, I gave the Ring-A-Ling pitch deck to him on a silver platter and wished him luck. When he made it to finals, I also lent him my ol' Lehman Brothers suit. Paul and Ring-A-Ling came in second place.

We took the news to my mentor, twenty-five-year Venture Capitalist Jim Armstrong, who'd been watching RideAmigos since we started almost six years earlier. Jim told us that if we built Ring-A-Ling, he'd invest the first $100,000.

Jim became our first angel investor.

It Pays to Give

Good things happen when I put myself out there in service to others. This story is not only cosmic in all of its coincidences, but it reinforces the inspiring paradox that in giving, we are not left empty, but rather we are made more whole.

Jeff Hoffman experienced an unexpected revelation that supports this powerful and important way of engaging with business and life in general.

With several of my companies we created a community fund. I often challenge people to do this because it creates exponential value that cascades beyond those directly involved. Every quarter, we would take a percentage of revenues, which ties the fund to the company's performance, achieving a triple bottom line. Each quarter, I would give the responsibility to the employees and say, "Go help someone in our community."

Back in my days at that corporate job, the United Way was one of the main recipients of corporate money. The company would put a little chart on the wall that showed how much we donated to the United Way, which was great, but as an employee, you don't feel connected to it, you don't feel that you have anything to do with that metric.

But if I give cash to my employees and empower them to go find someone to give this money to, it's a totally different experience. When we sold that company, I discovered afterwards that from the day we started the company, to the day I sold it, not one person that worked for me had ever quit. We had zero percent voluntary turnover. I started calling people and saying, "I don't know why that is, but I'd like to do it on purpose next time. Why does no one ever quit?" The community fund was one of the big reasons. Past employees expressed that they had never had a job where the owner of the company hands them money to reinvest in their local communities.

They went on to describe how it was incredibly motivating to be incentivized to engage in their own communities. The harder they worked, the more money the company made, and the more people they received to help. They spoke about the pride they felt when driving past the very people we helped on the way to work every day. That program was way more important to my employees than I ever thought it would be.

I believe that the universe gives back whatever energy you put into it. Good, bad, whatever…the universe will reward you with what you give it. Our employees started to notice that. Things come full circle when they're out there taking care of people. I tell my team, "It's people over profits. Always do the right thing by people, and the rest will sort itself out."

The way I see it: embracing a giving mindset has no downsides. It fosters strong, reciprocal relationships that benefit you, your network, your business, and the greater community. When Jeff realized he had achieved zero voluntary personnel turnover, it was a stunning moment that speaks to the value of the concept. Jeff's desire to build an ethos of giving back and community engagement brought back significant returns, not only to the business in the form of an eager, motivated workforce, but also elevated his employees' sense of purpose and satisfaction. Conscious entrepreneurship means embracing a holistic approach, where progress in one area ensures progress in another.

Make It Real: Your "Give, Give, Get" Challenge

Key Takeaways

- Generosity isn't just altruism—it's a way to create value for yourself and others.
- Giving can take many forms: time, knowledge, mentorship, opportunities, or even just a moment of encouragement.
- The more you give, the more you get. The universe (or the network of human expression) has a way of circling generosity back in unexpected ways.

Your Action Plan

- Identify your value. What skills, knowledge, or resources do you have that could benefit someone else? Write down three things you can offer today.
- Act on it. Over the next week, intentionally give something without expecting anything in return. It could be an introduction, advice, or a small act of service.
- Reflect and track. At the end of the week, reflect. Did an unexpected connection or opportunity arise? More importantly, how did it make you feel?

AI Prompt: "Based on my background in [industry/skills], give me three ways I could help others without asking for anything in return. Keep it authentic and high value."

MASTER THE PIVOT

"I see entrepreneurs afraid to make mistakes. They end up
paralyzed with indecisions. We made every mistake in the book.
We hired the wrong people. We didn't fire them fast enough. We
had the wrong pricing, we put the office in the wrong location...
But the goal is to make mistakes, learn, and move on quickly."

—Darren Berkovitz, co-founder of Telesign ($330 million exit)

When you start a company or a project, the initial idea at inception is rarely the same as the final version you end up with. "End" being a relative term as successful companies continue to evolve as time goes on to meet the changing needs of their consumer base. A famous example is Instagram.

Instagram: The Quick and Dirty version

Instagram was developed in San Francisco by Kevin Systrom and Mike Krieger. Systrom created a prototype app of an idea he originally called Burbn, which allowed people to check-in where they are on their mobile web app. They decided that the app was very similar to other already established mobile apps, so they pivoted to focus solely on communication through images. They stripped out all the features from the app except uploading photos, commenting, and liking. It was renamed Instagram which referred to the fact that users were sending a type of instant telegram.

Instagram launched on October 6th, 2010, and its growth was nearly instantaneous. From a handful of users, it soon became the number one photography app gathering one hundred thousand users in one week, increasing to one million in two months. According to Kevin Systrom, the app itself took only eight weeks to build but was a result of over a year of work behind it. It went on to be bought by Facebook for $1 billion in 2012.[1]

Instagram did not start as the Instagram we know and experience today, rather it was one feature within a greater check-in platform. The founders seized an opportunity by stripping down the app to focus on photo-sharing, which they noticed had become a popular feature among the Burbn users. Companies are constantly shape-shifting to find and meet the market and target their user base.

---

[1]   Eudaimonia, "How Instagram Started," Medium, January 26, 2017, https://obtaineudaimonia.medium.com/how-instagram-started-8b907b98a767.

One Pivot Often Leads to Another

When we originally launched Ring-A-Ling, it was an audio ringtone that you could push to your friends' phone when you called them—thus curating their experience. After our initial launch, Sohrab—our third co-founder and head of product— came in and suggested we make it a *video* ringtone instead. Genius. We'd call it, Vyng.

Feedback Is Key

Vyng is an Android-only app, and in order to test it, we needed to go where Android devices were prevalent. We found a heat map published online by Twitter that showed the geographic distribution of their Android and iPhone users at the time. Off to Riverside, California, we went, where the ratio was fifty/ fifty. We purchased Starbucks gift cards to hand out as incentives, walked around the mall, and onboarded passersby with Androids to download and try Vyng.

Unfortunately for us, the app wasn't working that well. Since we had only tested in Santa Monica where 4G was ubiquitous, we didn't know our app had problems when 4G wasn't readily available—this was a big "Aha!" moment. Riverside had slightly lower-end devices, bandwidth issues, and network conditions at the mall not seen in our testing environment.

This revelation led to the understanding that we needed more testing. Keep in mind that we had raised about $500,000 at this point, and we were almost out of money. But Vyng was building a global app, and we needed to go somewhere with even more Androids in varying conditions to accurately test and hone in on making a great product.

Tijuana or Bust

After looking at Android adoption across the globe, the closest Android-centric city on the map was Tijuana, Mexico, where the Android penetration was over 90 percent. The whole team hopped in a white rental van and sprang for the border. Four hours later, we met up with some friends of friends at a local university, who helped us using our original strategy to recruit students into downloading Vyng in exchange for five-dollar Starbucks gift cards.

The app wasn't working for any of them.

Many people had phones we'd never seen before—dual SIM card devices, phones with no data… "What's a video ringtone?" many people asked. "Do both people need to have the app?" Overall, Vyng was offering a complicated user experience, which is rarely what people are looking for. But we were learning quickly what needed to change, evolve, or drop entirely.

Back and forth to Tijuana we traveled for about a month, re-coding the app to prepare for conditions that mirrored the rest of the global Android market. At this point, we had $40,000 left in the bank, and the clock was ticking.

Late at night, on one of our long drives home, Sohrab turned to the rest of us and said, "Don't kill me, but I have a crazy idea…. What if we launched an app where every time you got a phone call, a fun cat video played as the video ringtone? That's it."

"You're a goddamn genius," I replied. We called it Purring. Get it? purrrr-ring!

...And Another Pivot

The technology was already built, and it was the simplest MVP that didn't require multiple people to have the app. This was a major pivot that would allow us to test the market, focus on a simple user experience, and target a very specific demographic—cat lovers.

From a longer-term strategy perspective, cat videos were one of many content channels that Vyng would offer—dogs, babies, music genres, dance, nature—all sorts of categories curate the tone of a phone call. Every time a user would get a call, a different video in the channel of their choice would play on the lockscreen as a video ringtone.

Each call became a test and a chance to learn. No story illustrates the power of rapid iteration better than what I heard in my interview with Stephen Kaufer, the co-founder and former CEO of TripAdvisor, which was acquired by Expedia in 2004 and later went public with a current market cap of $2 billion.

My wife and I went to a travel agent to plan a trip to Mexico. I got handed three brochures of different resorts: the inexpensive one, the moderately priced one, and the super luxury one. It was an easy decision for me; we're staying in the cheap one. But we took the brochures back home to discuss further. I married a smart woman because she said, "Why don't you go on the Internet and take a look?" I typed the name of the resort, and I got around a thousand hits.

"Awesome," I thought. But I quickly realized they were just random travel agencies from around the world that had scanned the same brochure I was looking at onto their websites. They had no opinions, no recommendations, nothing good, nothing bad—just a telephone number to call for a price if I wanted to stay there.

That wasn't useful, so I dove deeper. As a CS major, I was using Boolean logic in search engines to filter out anything with a fax number from a travel agency. I wanted someone's opinion, not a generic listing. Eventually, I found what was essentially a blog entry with pictures of their stay there, which showed me that I would be coming home divorced if we stayed there.

My wife and I mentally upgraded ourselves to that mid-priced one, went on the trip, and had a great time. When we came home, she said, "You're looking for another idea. Why not build a website that would help people find out what's good and bad about travel?" And I said, "Nah…" A year later, that was still the best idea that we had come up with.

I needed a B2C solution, but in late 1999, the dot-com bust was in full swing, and fundraising for an eyeball-driven B2C model wasn't a viable strategy. So, TripAdvisor was actually born as a B2B company, crawling the web to find insightful information about where you should go, where you should stay, and what you should do for every destination. Then serve it up to consumers using portals like Expedia, Yahoo, Travelocity,

AOL Travel, and other major travel sites. On that idea, my co-founders and I raised just over a million dollars.

We incorporated in February of 2000. By October of 2000, we had launched demo.tripadvisor.com. It was more like a vertical search engine for travel, linking to the sites that hosted the articles, blogs, guides, etc., from across the web. Then we went to market, "Hey, Expedia, do you want to sign up?" For a year, the answer was "no."

In the summer of 2001, we struck a deal with Lycos travel. We powered a lot of the content on their pages in exchange for a rev share on the CPM advertising that they sold.

Our first check from Lycos with our rev share payment was around five hundred dollars for ninety days. I wasn't worried because it was obviously a mistake, right? I called them up and inquired, and they confirmed it was correct.

I was naive at the time because we didn't know that when Lycos would sell a CPM ad, they wanted to keep 100 percent of the money. So, they'd run the ad on their wholly owned properties. The ads running on our pages were all house ads. We were getting 50 percent of nothing. Nail in the coffin. One of the biggest sites out there is generating zero revenue dollars. Getting five more of those deals won't change anything. And with 9/11, all the other B2B partnership pipelines dried up faster than anything I'd ever seen.

By October of 2001 we had a failed product, failed distribution channel, some traffic to the website, but nothing notable. And only about six months of runway left.

At that point, the team went from twelve people to nine after a mini layoff. I went to the board and offered back the little money we had left to our investors. The board casually said, "Steve, ten cents on the dollar back is not helpful for my fund. You guys are smart. Maybe you'll figure something out. Don't go bankrupt. Just do an orderly shutdown and give it a shot." Very smart on their part.

We tried many different iterations. We tried several that flat out did not work. I credit our eventual success, not to the brilliance of a brainstorming session laying out what could we do, but to the fact that the entire team was committed to trying as many of these ideas in sixty days as we could.

The first idea was simple: we were getting tens of thousands of visitors to our site through search engines and PR. I thought, "We're a travel website, so if I place an Expedia banner ad in a prominent position, our click-through rate will be at least ten to twenty times better than the standard 0.1 percent." We were in a hurry, so instead of calling Expedia to ask if we could sell them advertising, I took a screenshot of their banner ad, pasted it onto our site, and went live the next day. Sure enough, it didn't work. We got a 0.1 percent click-through rate. It didn't matter at all that we were a travel site. But the whole test was accomplished in literally less than a week. Tried it, didn't work. Onto the next.

Next, we tried to offer a directory-style integration. LookSmart had a directory where businesses were paying a couple hundred bucks to be listed in their directory every year. So, we built a little self-service payment model where you could list your hotel. The benefit is you'd get your URL and a phone number next to your hotel, so if a consumer liked what they read about it, they could call up to book it. Very easy value proposition. We called hotels and said, "Try this." They said, "No, never heard of you, and you have no traffic." That was for the hotels that we made it through to talk to in the first place. Second bad idea.

Eventually, the idea that worked was inspired by what goto.com did way back in the day or how Google ads work today. You're looking into booking the Marriott Copley Place Hotel in Boston. You see some reviews from a guidebook, a newspaper, and a blog post, and we put a very prominent link that said, "Check pricing availability for this Marriott on Expedia." No matter what the reviews say, if you can't afford it or it's not available, it's not a good hotel for you.

A lot of people clicked on that link. Not a tenth of a percent, not 1 percent, but 10 percent. Wow, that'll work! Now I just need to get someone to pay for it.

In November of 2001, we did a trial with Expedia where we sent them links for free that we tracked so they could understand the conversion. Then we nervously waited to see whether in December Expedia would pay for these clicks. The negotiation was pretty funny because they saw that some of these clicks convert, so they asked, "How much do they cost?" I was willing to take a nickel, but I know it's smarter to keep my mouth shut.

Instead, I asked what was the going rate for traffic like this. He said, "Around fifty cents." Which I'm sure was half of what it was really worth. But I was a strong negotiator [*said with sarcasm*] and said, "Done deal!" I knew the price would go up over time. More importantly, we had a client that was willing to pay.

By December of 2001, our first revenue month was $10,000. We had a low burn rate of around $80,000 a month, so we quickly grew traffic. We signed up one or two other travel agencies, and by March of 2002, we were profitable. We have grown profitably every quarter since then. In fact, we were profitable every quarter and we grew year in year out until COVID.

By April 2004, we sold the company for around $200 million in cash. At that point, we were generating about $50 million in revenue and over $20 million in profit. I stayed on as CEO.

Several people claim credit for the evolution from pulling in reviews to getting reviews from users, but we can't clearly identify who had the idea. It wasn't me. We listed links to guidebooks first, then newspapers and magazines, and then random comments on the web.

Someone said that we should add user reviews. So, we had a section at the very bottom that said, "Add your own comment." We looked at the click trail, and of all those pieces, people were more interested in the reviews than the guidebooks.

Seven, eight years later, guidebooks and magazines completely disappeared for lack of interest by consumers. By that time, we had a million reviews. As a consumer, you shouldn't trust one or two reviews of a hotel, but when you get to fifty or so, that's actually a broader insight than the one guidebook perspective by an experienced traveler.

It's hard to believe, but we were doing four hundred million visitors to desktop and mobile a month, and people come back time and again.

I advised entrepreneurs that if customers aren't willing to pay, either change the product or give up. If it's a distribution problem, pivot. At TripAdvisor, we shifted from B2B to B2C, testing multiple revenue models without a clear answer. I learned to be open to change, listening to others' feedback while staying open to adjusting ideas.

Stephen's story highlights the importance of adapting when a strategy isn't sustainable. That's all a pivot really is: the capacity to change to meet the challenges of the new moment before you. The unexpected gift was his investors giving him the go ahead to throw everything at the wall and see what sticks. He knew he had a product users liked; the idea was born from his own consumer experience. It was simply a matter of discovering a monetization strategy. The team didn't waste time waiting for a miracle; they tried many ideas in quick succession, each failing but giving them valuable insights for the next pivot. Being open to feedback and integrating new information, whether gained through failures or successes, is a key part of the pivot process.

Make It Real: Your "Master the Pivot" Challenge

Key Takeaways

- Pivots are inevitable. Whether you're launching a product or scaling a company, your initial idea will likely evolve.
- Embrace failure. Learn from your mistakes quickly. Every failure offers an opportunity to refine your approach.
- Feedback, feedback, feedback. Listen to your customers and the market. Refine your offering and discover new opportunities.

Your Action Plan

- Identify a potential pivot. Take a look at your current project or business.
  - What feedback have you received that could lead to a pivot?
  - Write down at least three changes you might make to your product, service, or business model to better meet your audience's needs.
- Test your idea. Identify a small, low-risk way to test your pivot idea.
  - Gather feedback from real customers.
  - Set a clear metric of success, and commit to iterating based on the results.

AI Prompt: "My business/project in [insert area] isn't getting the traction I want. Based on what's [working and what's not], give me three smart pivot options—one bold, one lean, and one unexpected."

PERFECT THE ELEVATOR PITCH

We built Purring in about a week. With money running out, we needed to get the word out and do something drastic… The month we launched it, there happened to be a cat convention (yes, you read that right) called CatCon in Los Angeles. Twenty-thousand cat lovers under one roof, and we were ready to win them over.

Your Elevator Pitch Matters

Once you have an idea, it's important to start talking about it. The elevator pitch is a fundamental element to nail down when starting a business. It's a succinct twenty to thirty second narrative that explains what you're working on in its most basic and total form.

It should be interesting, memorable, and tight.

The elevator pitch also needs to explain what makes you—or your organization, product, or idea—unique. One crazy way of practicing your elevator pitch is to literally get into an elevator and give one.

Pitching at CatCon

At CatCon, my co-founders and I took turns riding the elevator up and down. "Hi everyone, do you love cats? Awesome! We have a new Android app called Purring, and after you download it, every time you get a phone call, you experience a cute cat video on your lock-screen instead of a boring ringtone. You can download it today for free in the Google Play Store!"

Test, Tweak, Repeat

Each pitch was fifteen to thirty seconds, which is really all you need to sell cat videos to cat lovers. The frequency of elevator rides also offered the perfect landscape to tweak the pitch and see what landed with audiences. I rode the elevator up and down and eventually ended up meeting the founder of CatCon on one of the rides. An important reminder—when you're in High Five Energy flow and putting yourself out there, you never know who you're going to meet.

Not only is this a great way to practice your elevator pitch, it's also a greater tool to test and perfect how you talk about your project. Whether in an actual elevator, with friends and family, or in class—practice, practice, practice. Elevators are just one of many ways to secure a captive audience. And when you find yourself in them, leverage that opportunity.

Team photo.

The following story is from my interview with Brian Lee, an entrepreneur and investor best known for co-founding LegalZoom, ShoeDazzle, The Honest Company, and Arena Club.

My friend Brian Liu and I met in law school at UCLA. We both became attorneys. He ended up working at Sullivan & Cromwell, and I ended up working at Skadden Arps, both New York firms but here in LA. Every day at lunch we would dream up big ideas and try to find ways to start something on our own.

The first idea we came up with was called LawGarden, because we both liked the band Soundgarden. The concept was to create a platform where stay-at-home attorneys could provide legal advice online for ninety-nine cents a minute. However, the plan proved unfeasible for many reasons: It would still classify us as a law firm under existing regulations, and we'd have to pass the bar in all fifty states, which we didn't want to do. We had to consider fee-splitting rules and a lot of other rules. You couldn't raise capital from non-attorneys to start the company. So, there were many roadblocks to achieving that initial vision.

Then we shifted that idea from legal advice to legal documents. Basically taking what TurboTax did for tax returns and doing that for simple legal documents. That is how we came up with LegalZoom.com. Through R&D we found the right price and product market fit.

Now, when we started LegalZoom, in 1999 early 2000 range, it was the early days of the internet. People's number one concern was privacy. There was a general fear of the internet and fear of providing sensitive information like a credit card. Even though I had worked at Skadden, my business partner at Sullivan, two great firms, 99 percent of America had never heard of these firms, especially the mass consumer. We realized that we had to put a well-known attorney front and center.

Robert Shapiro was the most famous attorney in the world at the time, having just come off of the O. J. Simpson trial. So, I asked all my friends, "Do you know Robert Shapiro?" No one I knew was connected to him.

I eventually called 411 Information. This was before Google; you could call 411 and ask for a phone number.

I called and asked for Robert Shapiro, Attorney, Central City—and I got his phone number.

I remember it was 8:30 PM or so. I had a voice message written out that I expected to leave on his voicemail, and I called the number.

I didn't know this at that time, but he worked long hours. You can imagine my surprise when he actually picked up the phone and said, "Hi, this is Robert Shapiro. How can I help you?"

I said, "Robert Shapiro, the attorney?"

He said, "Yes."

And I said, "Well, my name is Brian Lee, and I have a business idea I'd like to run by you." I could tell he was just about to hang up on me and I said, "Wait! How do you know you're not interested if you don't hear me out?"

Hearing the desperation in my voice, he said, "You got two minutes."

In those two minutes, I laid out the entire idea for LegalZoom, integrating technology, using the internet to create legal documents and so forth.

At the end of those two minutes, he said, "What's your name again?"

I said, "Brian."

He said, "Brian, I'll tell you what. I was thinking something similar. Why don't you call tomorrow at a decent hour, and my assistant will set up a time for us to meet?" And that's how we met Robert Shapiro and started LegalZoom.

Every time he went on CNN and mentioned LegalZoom, we would get orders. That's when I realized the power of influence and celebrity.

LegalZoom is still doing great, today. It's a public business that is still profitable and still growing. It feels good to have started a company that hopefully will be around for another generation. That's the lesson I would share with other aspiring entrepreneurs: when your back is against the wall and you feel like there's no way out, you will find a way. You will find a way. When everyone said they didn't know Robert Shapiro, they couldn't make an introduction, I found a way.

Not only does this story bring me back to the suspense of my cold calling days at Lehman, but it flawlessly showcases the Hero's Journey of an entrepreneur: first, he became the solution, solving for the need to democratize access to basic legal documents. An idea born from his personal experience as an attorney. Then he iterated, pivoting until they found product market fit. Finally, he illustrated how a concise, compelling pitch can capture someone's attention and make magic. In this high-stakes scenario, Brian had mere moments to convey the essence and potential of LegalZoom to one of the most recognized attorneys in the world. By distilling his business idea into a clear, impactful message, he turned a cold call into a partnership that brought instant credibility and visibility to the company.

Make It Real: "Perfect the Elevator Pitch" Challenge

Key Takeaways

- Keep it concise. Twenty to thirty seconds is all you need.
- Make it memorable. Highlight what makes your idea unique.
- Test and refine: practice in real-world settings to see what resonates.

Your Action Plan

- Craft your pitch.
- Record yourself. Say it out loud and listen for clarity and impact.
- Test it live. Share it with three people (friends, colleagues, strangers), and note their reactions.
- Tweak and improve. Adjust based on feedback until it flows naturally.

AI Prompt: "Based on this business description [paste it] or this deck [summarize or link], write a thirty-second pitch that clearly explains what we do, why it matters, and what makes us different."

Bonus Challenge: Find an unexpected place—an elevator, coffee shop, networking event—and test your pitch in real time!

TAKE RISKS

Life is full of unsuspected opportunities to promote yourself or your project. These moments may not necessarily be curated ahead of time but nonetheless present a chance to engage.

Taking Center Stage

CatCon culminated in a sold-out Cat Video Awards show at the Ace Hotel Theater. Sohrab and I were standing in the aisle between the rows of seated convention-goers when we noticed that no one was on stage yet. Most of the people were still gathering and getting settled in their seats. We looked at each other, the same idea forming in our minds... "Do we dare?"

The audience comprised a sea of cat lovers, each with cell phones. We were still riding the high of having just pitched countless people in elevators and felt emboldened by how much fun we were having. Since we weren't trying to sell anything or burden anyone, we gave it a shot. We took a breath and walked onto the stage. "Hello and welcome to CatCon! Who loves cat videos?" (Insert heavily practiced elevator pitch here).

A sea of cat lovers.

Not surprisingly, the audience thought we were the sponsors for the entire event—I mean, we *were* in matching t-shirts. After our announcement, people started downloading the app. As the theater continued to fill with more people and because our performance was so well received, we pitched Purring a second time once every seat was taken.

This story is a short but relevant example of how seeing the world through a different lens—one of fun, play, and no rules—unlocks High Five Energy flow. What once seemed off-limits becomes an open stage—sometimes quite literally.

Rules Are Made to Be Broken

Rules begin at home, laid down by our parents. They are reinforced in schools where they are imperative to creating order in an environment of learning. As adults, those rules evolve into laws and the cycle of conditioning continues. The notion of following someone else's order is ingrained in our psyche from the day we are born. So, it makes sense that most people's first inclination is to stay in line and not talk out of turn. In the overarching sense, rules that ensure our safety and help us function as a cohesive society serve a vital purpose. But when it comes to creating something new, we must remember that in the end, rules are just made up by other people. And *sometimes* rules are meant to be broken.

Some days later, the founder of CatCon messaged me on Facebook, saying that Vyng's impromptu participation was quite fun and entertaining. It shows that our risk, if nothing else, brought joy to cat lovers in the audience. As you go through life, remain open to creating these opportunities that are both joyous and beneficial toward your endgame.

No Risk, No Reward

Taking risks also means putting it all on the line if you believe that you have an opportunity to succeed. Our last story from my interview with Jeff Hoffman hits the nail on the head, showcasing the idea that taking risks is a vital part of the game.

When we first created the ticketing kiosks, you were not allowed to access the data from the back office of airline systems in any way, shape, or form; it was strictly off-limits. By the time we got to Priceline years later, APIs had been developed, allowing third-party developers to write code that connected to airline reservation and hotel systems. But back then, none of that existed.

So we had to do something really bold. The only way to get a connection to the airline and hotel mainframes back then was through certified travel agents, licensed through IATA [the International Air Transport Association]. With that, you could order one terminal that connected to the airline mainframe.

So, I figured, "Let's just hire a travel agent." Never mind that we weren't actually a travel agency. Even the travel agent we hired was confused, saying, "Where's the travel agency?"

And I said, "Don't worry about that. The legal requirements of the contract is, 'We have to have a travel agent on payroll.' You're on payroll. You can go get another job now."

When the airline's techs came to install our connection to their system, they asked similar questions like, "Where are the brochures?" We played along, let them set up the connection. Then stripped the cover off the terminal and wired it straight into our server farm and started pulling data out of the back office. Suddenly, we had real-time access to airline data—something no one outside the industry had ever pulled off.

Eventually, they called me and said, "I'm pretty sure if it's not a civil lawsuit, you're going to jail." I pointed out that it's not actually a law. They had just never anticipated somebody doing this. I asked how they caught on, and he said, "You either have a thousand travel agents typing two million words a minute, or you're taking this data, which we've never seen before."

It was pretty dangerous and a bold move, but I said, "We're downloading your data."

Silence.

Then, "You're probably going to jail."

Instead, we signed partnerships with every major airline.

Taking risks is embedded in the fabric of the entrepreneurial landscape. If you think about it, any deviation from a prescribed norm is a risk because we don't yet know the outcome. In order to create something new, you'll need to tread uncharted waters. Jeff saw the barrier around strict airline backend restrictions, and instead of accepting it as an immovable obstacle, he found a loophole and dove in headfirst, knowing there could be serious consequences. Jeff's rule breaking ended up redefining the industry. Because sometimes, breaking the rules is just seeing the future before everyone else.

Make It Real: Your "Take Risks" Challenge

Key Takeaways

- Opportunities often arise in unexpected places. Be ready to seize them.
- Rules are often just conventions set by others. Question them.
- Taking risks can lead to breakthroughs, even when it feels uncomfortable.

Your Action Plan

- Think of one idea, project, or opportunity you've hesitated to pursue because of a "rule"—whether that's a workplace norm, social expectation, or industry standard.
- Ask yourself: Who made this rule? What would happen if I broke it?
- *If* breaking the rule doesn't break the law (or hurt anyone), then let's go for it.
- Take one small, bold action this week to push against that boundary.

AI Prompt: "I'm thinking about taking a risk in [insert area] with [background context]. Help me play out the best-case scenario, worst-case, and most likely outcomes—and what I'd do in each case."

LEVERAGE WHAT'S AVAILABLE

How do we keep the momentum from CatCon going? We knew we needed a video ad that could tell our story and get people's attention—and we had no budget.

Constraints Fuel Creativity

My friends and I held a clothing swap in the living room of my home once a year for a few years running. Everyone brought clothing they were giving away and could take items from other people's castoffs. With everyone in one place (you know me by now), I took advantage of the opportunity. I asked if the group would mind shooting a short commercial for Vyng.

Sohrab came over and set up his camera and some basic lighting in the living room. Utilizing not only our friends, but the donations as well, I asked everyone to grab something fun from the pile of clothes and props. We had guitars, roller skates, and a monster head. We asked our friend Veronica—already in attendance—to be the main actress. We didn't go out and hire anybody. We simply worked with what he had, extras and all.

The Commercial

Sohrab came up with the concept of Veronica leaning in to answer a normal phone call with the black lock screen. When a cat video played in place of the generic, lifeless ringtone, a raucous reaction from all in attendance would illustrate the awesome nature of a video ringtone. We buttoned the ad with Sohrab's voice saying, "Make your ringtonessssssss, cats!"

No Need to Break the Bank

We placed the commercial on Facebook and targeted people who like cats, which is a surprisingly significant portion of the planet. The response was overwhelming.

In all, we launched Purring at CatCon, posted the app to the website Product Hunt, and published a fun Facebook ad with a video we shot in my living room. Two weeks after that, we had one hundred thousand cat videos playing a day. Based on the success of Purring and the proof of concept of channels, we raised another $500,000. Vyng survived to live another day.

Eventually, that little video for Purring would become the base video template for all of our promotional content. Our secret sauce was using that same commercial and simply replacing the cat video ringtone with other channels of content—dance, adventure, Bollywood, and more—and targeting Facebook users who liked *that* category. The result was highly targeted advertising campaigns getting downloads for less than one penny per user.

The key takeaway is recognizing the value of the resources at your disposal and leveraging them to create success for yourself. We shot the commercial with a standard smartphone camera, a few friends, and a creative idea. Because of the targeted marketing, we were able to scale up really quickly—that commercial has now been seen tens of millions of times. Oftentimes, limitations ignite creativity. It's with creative problem-solving that a lack of resources becomes your advantage.

A Viral Video Changed the Industry

The following is a story from my interview with Mike Dubin, an entrepreneur best known for founding Dollar Shave Club, acquired by Unilever for $1 billion in 2016.

When I was living in New York probably in 2007, 2008, I recognized that it was a pain in the ass to buy razors. I was on the subway platform right near Duane Reade at Rockefeller station. I don't even know if the Duane Reade is still there, but I was standing outside the Duane Reade thinking, "I don't want to go in because I don't want to wait in the line." They were expensive, and I couldn't just get my own razor blades myself, I had to find the person with the key to the locked fortress where they keep them behind, et cetera.

So I observed the problem back then, but I didn't do anything with it, yet. Then a few years later in 2011, I bumped into my friend's father who was an importer of sorts and had a bunch of different products, cake slicers, razors, a few other things. I said to him, "I'll take the razors off your hands." I knew exactly what I wanted to do with them. Offer a direct-to-consumer subscription service for razors where customers could sign up for a monthly subscription and receive razor blades delivered straight to their door at a lower price than traditional retail brands

Next, we filmed a video that is still online today—you can see it. I wrote it myself drawing on my experience as a student in sketch and improv comedy. Then I reached out to a friend of mine, Lucia, who went on to direct *Hacks*, and *Broad City*, and a few other things. She had just moved to LA, and I said, "Hey, will you direct this?" And she said, "Sure, no problem." We had a very small budget of $4,500, and we shot the video in one day—an achievement in itself.

We launched the video on March 6th, 2012, and it went viral and put us on the map, which you couldn't have planned. Its success was bolstered by a well-executed PR push tied to our launch and our first million-dollar fundraise, along with the added bonus of a slow news day.

Dollar Shave Club's 2012 launch video, titled "Our Blades Are F***ing Great," became one of the most famous viral marketing campaigns in history. This story perfectly illustrates the value in "Leveraging What's Available." The initial inconvenience of buying razors sparked the idea, but the real breakthrough came from utilizing existing resources: razors from a friend's father, a small $4,500 budget, personal skills in comedy and writing, and the directorial talent of a friend. By maximizing what was readily available—resources and connections—the team created a viral video that generated twelve thousand orders in the first forty-eight hours. I love this story because it emphasizes how strategic use of limited resources can propel creativity and drive progress.

Make It Real: Your "Leverage What's Available" Challenge

Key Takeaways

- Leverage existing resources: The tools, connections, and opportunities we need are often already at our disposal.
- Limitations ignite creativity: When you have less to work with, it becomes a forcing function for creative solutions.
- Get creative: Think outside the box.

Your Action Plan

- Identify one outcome you want to accelerate this month—product, audience, revenue, or something else.
- Search for AI tools or no-code platforms that can replace or compress the next three steps you'd normally do manually.
- Run a real experiment using one of those tools this week—even if it's rough. Document what it unlocks.

AI Prompt: "I'm working on [insert project or business idea]. What are three AI tools or agents I could use to automate, test, or build faster—especially for solo founders or lean teams?"

FIND YOUR CHAMPION

Months passed and as initially planned, we added more and more content channels to Vyng. From every type of music genre to our classic cat videos, dozens of options filled the app. Eventually, users could upload their own videos to a public library that anyone could search and assign as their video ringtone. Combined with our epic Facebook ad made in my living room, the app was going viral.

Series A

With almost three hundred million video ringtones played within the app, three hundred thousand monthly active users, and 21 percent week over week growth, it was time to raise our Series A. While our metrics were really strong, we came up against some major challenges pitching venture capital firms in LA, SF, and NY:

- Vyng was Android only, and 99 percent of US investors had an iPhone.
- There were 80 percent of our users coming from India. At the time, the general sentiment in the US was that we could not monetize Indian users.
- Vyng is built on phone calls. "Phone calls, who makes phone calls anymore?" was the most frequent response.

I think it's worth mentioning that Vyng was eager to integrate into the iPhone universe, but as many know, iPhone is a walled garden, and the permissions didn't (and still don't) exist to allow outside apps to access the lock screen.

Needless to say, finding a VC to get on board was not easy. Lots of pitches, lots of nos. What was crazy is that our lead investor from the first round, March Capital, had experience in India, and was willing to participate in the round—but they wanted another large institutional venture capital firm to lead, and we could not find one. "Leading a round" means being the primary investor in a funding round. This investor typically sets the terms of the deal (valuation, investment structure, and other factors) and often invests the largest amount of money. We needed to find a champion who believed in us and the Vyng vision.

Follow the Users…to India!

One day, we realized that if our users are in India, then perhaps our investors should be, too. We purchased four tickets to India and began networking. Leveraging every relationship we had, we started making virtual pitches prior to our departure date to qualify leads. Our story was resonating, and one meeting by one meeting we began building out a massive itinerary.

Using the anchor meeting strategy (see Ch. 33)—telling people we'd be in a city before we had set plans, "Hey, I'll be in New Delhi Jan 16–19, want to meet?"—we crushed it. Plus, we did have the *Hot American App in Town* aura working to our benefit. We had amassed over thirty in-person meetings—enough to justify the expense of the trip, and we took off on our first adventure to India: nine days, three cities.

An Emerging Market

Not only did we meet investors, but we met our user! There is *nothing* more valuable when building a product than speaking with your customers. Why was Vyng so popular in India? Well, allow me to tell you.

1. Up until recently, India was mostly a 3G network speed country. Then the massive oil and gas conglomerate Reliance, owned by the richest man in India, decided to spend $6 billion dollars to put up 4G towers across the country and launch Reliance Jio. Almost overnight, data rates plummeted to one of the cheapest in the world, and a half billion people were projected to be going from feature phones to smartphones. Today, Jio has over 460 million mobile subscribers.

2. Ringtones are still a thing! From investors to taxi drivers, everyone has a custom ringtone. Everyone. We realized that the iPhone had killed the ringtone in the US

since it made it so difficult to change the tune. India was 91 percent Android.

3. Vyng brought Bollywood videos to the lockscreen. Bollywood is like a religion in India. People across all demographics, ages, and geographies are obsessed with both the films and stars.

4. Regardless of what investors thought, people still made phone calls. Our users in India made twelve to fifteen calls per day.

All of those factors came together to create the ideal circumstances that allowed for Vyng's success. We could not have predicted this, but India was the perfect marketplace for a video ringtone app.

Get Ready for Your "Nos"

While many of the investors agreed and validated the synergetic moment, agreeing didn't mean they were going to write us a check for a million dollars. Keep in mind, many investors hear up to one hundred pitches per week and only invest in a handful of companies a year. For a fund to write a large check, a lot of factors need to align: being at the right stage, valuation, sector, and check size, to name just a few.

Get used to someone saying no, and DO NOT TAKE IT PERSONALLY. You never know what's happening inside a fund—internal politics, past experiences of investments, fund targets for investing in industry sectors—all of it outside of your control.

It Just Takes One Yes

In the beginning, we averaged one yes for every forty to fifty pitches. But here's the good news: you only need one yes. One champion, positioned internally at a fund—who believes in your vision, value proposition, and your team—to go to bat for you. The same goes for getting a job offer or landing a new customer—you need one champion to convince the rest of their peers that you are worth betting on.

On this trip, we found our champion in a partner at Omidyar Network, a global fund started by Pierre Omidyar, the founder of eBay. Omidyar had a Mumbai office focused on "the next half billion." They were truly a perfect match for Vyng.

It's Like Dating

I'm probably not the first person to make this analogy, but finding investors is very much like dating. *Both* sides have to fall in love. So just because someone offers you money, it does not mean you take it. Omidyar expressed interest in moving forward, and he asked us to have lunch in New Delhi on our last day of the trip so we could have a second "date" before heading home. We were in Bangalore at this point, 1.5 hours from the airport, five hours from Delhi, and our flight would be leaving from Bangalore the next day. If we did have this lunch, we would have to travel for almost twenty-four hours straight.

As Matthew Kidman says in the film *The Girl Next Door*, "The juice is worth the squeeze." We sucked it up and went for it. To make it manageable, we decided to congratulate one another with a handshake after every win. Getting into the taxi on time, arriving at the airport, passing through security—I mean every win was followed with a congratulatory handshake. Acknowledging small accomplishments on such a harrowing journey started to snowball; our spirits lifted, and magic was in the air. We absolutely crushed the meeting with Omidyar.

Afterward, while telling March Capital the good news of Omidyar's interest, we expected nothing more than a pat on the back until something concrete was secured. To our surprise, March was so impressed with our drive, feedback from the trip, and investor traction, they offered to lead our Series A with a $4 million investment at a $16 million pre-money valuation. Meaning, after we receive the cash, our company would be worth $20 million.

Victory! And we earned it. After weeks of further diligence, Omidyar Network co-invested $1 million, and we oversubscribed the round.

Your Champion Awaits

Your champion is out there. It may take fifty meetings and a trip across the world, but if you believe in your capacity to create what you need, you will find yours. And don't forget to celebrate the little wins along the way, as life is about the journey—the end goal is just a target.

A great example of "Finding Your Champion" is another story from my interview with Scott Dudelson. The story of Prodege, the parent company of Swagbucks.com, is packed full of archetypal stages experienced in his entrepreneurial journey. Prodege sold for over $1 billion.

Whenever I tell people "search engines," they say they never click on sponsored results, but it's like clockwork: five percent of searches will end up as sponsored result clicks.

So, it was never a matter of whether or not this idea would make money. It was a question of how much money will this idea make? And that always depended on the distribution. If the nonprofits brought users to us, we would make money. So, in the early days, back in 2005/2006, it was past the internet bust. Things online were starting to pick up again, but nonprofits are very slow to grasp how to raise money online.

After pitching a lot, we did get a few nonprofits on board, but it was like pulling teeth. There was this fundamental misunderstanding of how it works and how they were to promote it.

Out of the sites we partnered with, some were making eight dollars a month, maybe twelve dollars. At first glance, that seems horrible and nothing to write home about. However, I looked at it as proof of concept: this works. If we can scale, it'll be like clockwork.

At a certain point, we realized the nonprofits were not going to offer the distribution we needed. With my background being in the music industry, I had a lot of contacts through the nonprofit fundraising I was doing. I thought that maybe we should get the bands involved. We will create branded search engines for the bands.

How it worked: it would essentially be like a Google search engine but branded to a band like Maroon 5. Maroon 5 would tell their fanbase to use the site to do their online searches. We added a special twist to incentiv-ize fans: search the web and win rewards. Like autographs, earn a meet-and-greet with the band, etc. That was how we'd get people using the platform, which we needed.

Our network eventually expanded to include nearly two hundred sites at its peak. Some notables include Beyoncé, the New York Giants, World Wrestling Entertainment, and the Green Bay Packers. We started making real money. We saw that when World Wrestling Entertainment promotes this, or KISS promotes this, we could make a thousand dollars a day. They were able to funnel more users to the sites, validating its efficacy.

We continued this route for about two years—and it was good. We operated with a very lean team, so it was probably six of us and the company was making a few million dollars a year. But over time, what we realized was that the incentives of my company and the incentives of the bands were not aligned.

A sports team or a band, their business is selling music, selling tickets, selling merchandise. It's not pro-moting a search engine. It was tangential to what they do. Over time, there'd be a lot of attrition, because we'd, for example, run out of prizes. Or, artists would go out of cycle, because when an artist releases a record, they want to promote it. But when they go off tour, and they don't have a record to promote, they get quiet. Therefore, the last thing they want to promote is our search engine. As time went on, we started making less money. The only way to get revenue back up was to sign on more bands, more sports teams, which we could have done, but we knew that there was no long-term strategy. You gotta survive long enough to find the right thing.

We need to pivot this again to figure out how to maximize its potential. We know people want free stuff, but we needed to find something that's sustainable and that would allow us to control our destiny. The big realization was to create the same exact product that we had built for the bands; instead of earning Beyoncé autographs, you could earn points to redeem for Amazon gift cards or PayPal cash. That's it. We called it Swagbucks.

Within months of launching, it took off like a rocket ship. That was the pivot that really allowed us to break free and create massive success.

But that initial success was due in large part to mommy bloggers. For context, in mid-2008 is when we launched the Swagbucks product. And it coincided right when the economy crashed, and the stock market tanked. People were losing jobs. It was a pretty rough time. We had this product that allowed you to do what you're doing every day—searching the web—and get paid for it. That value proposition was appealing. After we launched, we started looking at the analytics. If you have a product or anything, you live and die by your analytics, on who's referring traffic to you.

We discovered it was Money Saving Mom bloggers who were referring us to their communities. At the time, mommy blogging was just blogs where moms could exchange resources: like how to get free diapers for their children because families were struggling. So, I contacted them and asked, "Where did you even come across

Swagbucks?" Turns out, they used to use the Wynonna Judd search engine through our network and eventually found Swagbucks. They mentioned that this was a way in which people could actually pay for the things they needed for their children.

I forged a relationship with them, and then over the next two or three months, every day there'd be a new mommy blog referring traffic to us. As other blogs started promoting us as well, it snowballed. Within the first year of launching Swagbucks, I don't remember the exact numbers, but we went from doing something like two million a year to fourteen million. The Money Saving Mom blogs still exist... I owe them a lot.

Finally, one of the biggest moves and game changers in our business came in 2014. We hadn't raised any real money. We bootstrapped Swagbucks, becoming a hundred-million-dollar company without raising any real capital. It was extraordinary. We decided to head up to Silicon Valley to meet all the big VCs. But it was very demoralizing. We went up there with a lot of confidence: we knew we had this amazing business that we built without outside help; it's churning out profit...but once we got up there, we were shunned.

People did not either understand the product or they took one look at me—with my big beard, really long hair and sandals—and my genius partner who also didn't fit the Silicon Valley pedigree, and didn't want to get involved with us. We both don't fit that mold.

We finally had a meeting at Technology Crossover Ventures where Chuck Davis was in the room. He was one of the firm's partners, and after we finished with our pitch, he came up to us and said, "I don't know if this team will invest. This isn't necessarily in their wheelhouse." Before we even had a chance to get discouraged, he continued to say, "I get this. I know what you're doing. I like you guys and this is real."

Chuck was the former CEO of Fandango and the former CEO of Shopzilla, both sold for five hundred-plus million. He was legit. He was one of the first people in this whole entire fundraising process who understood what we were doing and wanted to help us get to the next level.

We met back in LA, and he started digging into our business to see how he could help. He saw we needed to beef out our operations, so he brought on his former team including a CFO, a CTO, and HR department— skilled people who had grown and scaled companies before; truly transforming our business. Then ultimately Chuck, being very involved at this point, became CEO, bringing in investors with his new position. That led us to getting our first investment with Technology Crossover Ventures in 2014.

Later that year, after the investment from Technology Crossover Ventures, I officially stepped away from the company to focus on other passions. I kept some skin in the game, knowing the immense value of what Yosef and I had built. We'd created a powerful revenue machine, rich with data. Chuck and Yosef recognized that, when properly structured, this data held even greater potential. Over the next several years, they continued to scale the company relentlessly and built very profitable new product lines. By 2021, their efforts paid off when they sold it for over a billion dollars to private equity.

After two major pivots, first from his partnership with non-profits, then from branded search engines, Scott and his partners landed on a universally appealing model of offering gift cards and cash rewards to anyone. But the real breakthrough came when they discovered *mom bloggers* were organically promoting Swagbucks. The mom bloggers, acting as a champion within his user-base, helped catapult their business through digital word-of-mouth. Instead of passively benefiting from their promotion, Scott actively cultivated relationships with these bloggers and nurtured their support. Finally, they found their final champion in Chuck Davis, who saw the potential in the business, even when other people dismissed it. His involvement became a catalyst for growth, validating the founders' vision and attracting critical resources. The company evolved into a powerhouse, proving that the right champion can be the key to scaling effectively and achieving extraordinary success.

Make It Real: Your "Find Your Champion" Challenge

Key Takeaways

- You don't need a hundred yeses—just one champion who truly believes in your vision.
- Rejection is inevitable. Persistence and strategic positioning are essential.
- Understanding your market (even when others don't) can give you an edge.
- Relationships matter. Investors, customers, and advocates all play a role in your success.

Your Action Plan

- Identify your goal. What are you currently trying to achieve that requires a champion? (e.g., fundraising, landing a key client, career advancement)
- List ten potential champions. These could be investors, mentors, customers, or industry insiders who have the skills/influence to help you.
- Map your connections. Who in your existing network (even loosely) can help introduce you to these people? What creative strategies can you use to get in front of them?
- Build your outreach plan. Craft a strategy to engage with at least three potential champions this week—whether through a warm introduction, cold outreach, or showing up where they are.

AI Prompt: "I'm trying to connect with [name of person] to help with [goal]. Help me write a short, sincere message I can send—one that clearly explains what I'm building, why it matters, and how they could support or advise me."

Bonus: As you execute, celebrate the small wins. Each conversation, each connection, and each lesson learned is a step toward victory. Your champion is out there, you just have to find them.

Want to watch the full interview with Scott Dudelson?
Visit: www.jeffreychernick.com

EXPECT A ROLLER COASTER

Vyng evolved from video ringtones into a next-generation visual caller ID platform that made incoming calls from friends, family, and businesses more dynamic and recognizable—while filtering out spam and unverified numbers.

At this point, we've played over five billion caller ID videos across 170 countries and have a database of one billion unique contacts. When a user receives a visual ID from a business, call answer rates increase from 25 percent to 70 percent. That is *huge* when it comes to driving customer engagement for companies in delivery, banking, insurance, travel, and telehealth.

Vyng was driving the future of phone calls, and that future was looking bright.

Make Vyng Ubiquitous

As Vyng continued its growth, we continued to innovate on the lockscreen. Simultaneously, we were filing for lockscreen patents in the US, China, India, South Korea, Europe, and Canada. Eventually it became clear to the management team that in order for Vyng to truly be omnipresent, we had to integrate directly into the phone.

So, we created an office in New Delhi, India, where our user base resided, and began a year-long journey to build a software development kit (SDK), that could be installed into the device itself. This would ensure that when a person buys a Vyng-powered mobile phone, visual phone calls and messages would be part of the core user experience from the onset of the device—no downloads required. This was our thesis from the jump: that Vyng's technology was an inevitable future.

A New CTO

We needed a new CTO that understood the Indian market. A recruiter introduced us to GK who was working as a top engineering manager at a global company. Best case scenario, he would consider advising us. He agreed to meet us for coffee on his corporate campus in SF. After spending four hours walking around the different cafeterias, he declined becoming our CTO. But he did invite us to his cousin's wedding in Rajasthan, India. Little did he know he was inviting the Vyng crew—an unstoppable force when it came to doing whatever it takes to succeed.

We hopped on a plane and flew twenty-four hours to attend a glamorous, traditional, three-day wedding extravaganza. By the end, he was so impressed with how we showed up, he agreed to become our CTO. Here is the Vyng team in full fashion at the wedding.

GK led the effort to build out our New Delhi office, and we started to network our way into the OEM world (original equipment manufacturer), a.k.a. the folks that build the phones.

The Holy Grail of Distribution

After months of pitching and presenting, Samsung India was interested in integrating Vyng into thirty million devices, and OPPO India wanted to start with ten million. This was the holy grail of distribution.

Finalizing these deals from Los Angeles was proving to be difficult. So, when the head of the Samsung team offered to grab lunch and get to the finish line, it didn't matter that we were about to embark on a twenty-four-hour commute for lunch.

"The juice is worth the squeeze," right? Paul and I jumped on a flight and in March of 2020, we made it to the one yard line

with both Samsung and OPPO in negotiations for the integrations. We were literally having pizza with the OPPO team at their headquarters in Hyderabad, talking about presenting on stage during their big OS launch, when I got a phone call...

COVID

My sister, a doctor at NewYork-Presbyterian/Columbia University Irving Medical Center, called and strongly suggested I return home early. There was something happening in Italy called COVID-19, and she was worried I would get stuck in India. It was a hard choice at the time; we were *so* close to making video ringtones synonymous with phone calls, but I decided to heed her advice and return home before we could ink the deals. Two weeks later, India shut down for months. Businesses closed, people were forced to stay in their homes, the world came to a screeching halt—and so did our partnerships.

For the next eighteen months, the deals stalled. With no boots on the ground in India and a global pandemic causing uncertainty, our relationships struggled. Eventually Google took the OPPO deal by offering forty cents per mobile user, and Hiya, a caller ID provider, expanded its relationship from Samsung HQ to India. Our deals were done. And Vyng was dumped.

The Rollercoaster: Universal Experience of a Founder

The following story is from my interview with Edward Shenderovich, an entrepreneur, investor, and poet, who is recognized for his significant contributions to the technology and bioeconomy sectors. His roller coaster experience with the founding and selling of Knotel, a flexible office space provider that was positioned to transform the commercial real estate industry, also takes place during the landscape of COVID.

I was walking around Manhattan and thinking to myself that every one of these tall buildings, if a building is forty stories or higher, is a billion-dollar business. It's like you're walking around these unicorns sticking out of the ground. I thought, *This is the isle of unicorns.*

Historically, in order to build a billion-dollar technology company, it requires you to raise hundreds of millions in capital. The economics of these buildings seemed to follow a similar path. In the moment of creation, I think real estate developers are like venture entrepreneurs. It takes a vision to see a parking lot and imagine that it will be transformed into a hundred-story building. I thought, *Maybe I can bring something from this strange world of software into the world of real estate.* The word "prop tech" didn't exist then, so we called it "real estate tech." At first, I explored companies to invest in. I discovered WeWork, which at the time had maybe a billion-dollar valuation. At the same time, we were building a software company, and the vision for Knotel started to emerge.

We rented an office that was a little larger than what we needed, so we sublet a part of the office to another company. I spoke to my partner, Amol, about the potential of this idea saying, "We're doing nothing, and we're actually making money." We started iterating on what that idea could be…. We came to the idea that Knotel could provide space to growing teams, not to individuals. WeWork was already catering to the individual entrepreneur, selling solo office space in a community environment. We would be different. We would service companies, helping growing teams succeed. They need a space to work, and we will figure out a way to deliver that space to them.

In the very beginning, the first space we had to rent was our own excess office space, but it was difficult to sign new leases. Our first problem to solve was simply a matter of getting more space. You needed to be a credible tenant to sign a lease. In those early days, we leveraged what was immediately available to us and built out our inventory of office space with large subleases.

Actually, one of our first investors gave us a sublease on their own office space. That gave us credibility to procure more inventory of real estate: we could show that we're not only in this puny building in Flatiron, where we have a floor or two, but we also have a floor in a building in Fidai, a large skyscraper. Leveraging that, we got another building on Houston Street. Then we found out that one of the companies I was involved with was downsizing. We acquired half of their space, the whole floor on Cooper Square.

We achieved product market fit immediately. We started growing in New York, expanded to San Francisco and London, and continued growing from there. Then we bought a company in France, which is super successful and still the leading French flex office operator.

Things snowballed, and we ultimately got to about sixty locations in New York and in total more than two hundred locations globally. Things were really looking good.

Fast forward to early 2020: expansion is on the horizon, then COVID happens. All of a sudden, our customers are not able to access our product. Who could have foreseen that office spaces would not be available and accessible. We were in the office space business and companies and/or governments weren't letting people go into their offices for the foreseeable future. Not everywhere in the world was as strict as the US, but it was essentially the same outlook in all the countries where we were operating. In the US, however, the "stay at home" order persisted the longest. We very quickly realized that the status quo had changed.

In order to survive, we needed to freeze some of the operations. We unfortunately needed to let go of people immediately. That didn't feel great. We let go of all the people that were dealing with new office construction and the people that were dealing with the real estate side of the business. There simply was no business for these people to continue working on.

Over the course of the company's lifespan, we raised about $400 million in total, some of which was raised during the pandemic. But the real kicker was that we had a $100 million dollar investment deal scheduled to close on February 29th, 2020.

But over the course of a couple weeks, they started to slow things down, citing the uncertainties around a future with COVID. The company was not in a super great position cash-wise because we were growing, and we needed to acquire more space and figure out how to attract customers, but then that cash didn't come.

Ultimately, they rescinded the offer, expressing their apologies and attributing their inability to commit to our vision due to the uncertainty surrounding COVID. The months kept going by, and it wasn't until August that we were able to pull together another round. Things seemed to be turning a corner. As we were about to sign, Omicron happened. This much larger fund, who was slated to lead this new round, decided to wait as well.

The pandemic was like war. Every day I imagined people in a sort of combat, managing this immense psychological pressure, having no idea what's going to happen the next day. My main concern wasn't for what was happening to me, but what was happening to the people around me…. How will they react, how resilient are they? What's going on with them, their families? Will they show up at work—meaning, on Zoom—the next day? And if they're not showing up on Zoom, what's happened to them?… For many people, this felt like the end of the world. And Zoom is the ultimate sensory deprivation environment, siloing us within our little bubbles for a year…. It was a really strange time. I think we still haven't fully assessed what the impact of the pandemic was on us all.

By 2021, we found ourselves sitting on a significant amount of debt and needed to refinance. One of our shareholders stepped in and refinanced it in a way that ultimately resulted in ownership of the company shifting to them. They executed this by steering the company through bankruptcy and then purchasing the assets as a lender. That's how the company was sold in January

JEFFREY CHERNICK WITH ALIX GITTER

2021. At its peak, we employed over five hundred people, but by the time it was acquired, we were down to around two hundred.

Edward's story truly is a roller coaster, marked by exhilarating highs and gut-wrenching lows. I'm struck by the scope and imagery as he recounts walking around Manhattan, having an epiphany while looking at the towering buildings. Seeing the parallels between real estate and tech startups, particularly the entrepreneurial spirit that drives both industries, Edward discovered a way to innovate within the sector. The early days of Knotel reflect the entrepreneurial hustle of problem-solving and leveraging available resources to scale rapidly. Then COVID: the beginning of a new era, one that impacted so many businesses, communities, and lives. The crushing realization that this massive, well-built machine was suddenly teetering on the edge is heavy. You pivot, you adapt, and you try to hold it all together. But when the storm is that big, there are limits to what anyone can do. I think it's also worth mentioning that Knotel sold for around $70 million and is still a successful business today under its new ownership—proving its merit as a great idea.

Make It Real: Your "Embrace the Ride" Mindset

Key Takeaways

- The ride is inevitable. No matter how well you plan, there will be moments that push you to your limits and force you to adapt.

- Adaptability matters. Whether it's technology or market forces, the ability to adjust to external challenges can make the difference between success and failure.
- Shit happens.

When Things Feel Overwhelming:

- Name the chaos. Write down what feels overwhelming right now. What's actually happening—and what's just noise in your head?
- Move or make something. Choose one small act of creation or motion:
  - Take a fifteen-minute walk (no phone)
  - Doodle, journal, or cook something simple
  - Do anything that reminds you you're in control of your energy
- Zoom out. Ask:
  - What would future me say about this moment?
  - What's one thing I can control today?

Why It Works: Getting out of your head—and into your body, your breath, or a small act of creation—can snap you out of panic mode. From that calmer place, decisions get clearer. Energy gets cleaner. You remember: this isn't forever. You're still the one steering.

AI Prompt: "I'm feeling overwhelmed by [brief situation]. Help me calm down, reframe it, and remind myself what's actually in my control."

NOTHING DIES UNTIL YOU SAY SO

"You fire every bullet in the gun. Then you throw the gun.
And then you go hand to hand, and you don't quit until
somebody shows up and drags you out of there."

—Eric Salwan, co-founder of Firefly ($7 billion market cap)

The SDK plan was a great idea, but the landscape had changed.
I'm not going to lie, things were looking bleak for Vyng, and we
were losing morale. We needed a new plan if we were going to
make something happen. We decided to build a rewards system
on top of Vyng that let users earn tokens for performing actions
on the lockscreen. As crypto was making headlines across the
globe, we had our next big idea.

Resilience: A New Plan

Android mobile users everywhere could now earn bitcoin for something they're already doing—making phone calls to friends, family, and businesses. That's the value proposition behind the Bitcoin Dialer, Vyng's newest feature.

By this time, Vyng had been issued nineteen lockscreen patents in the US and one patent in China. Word of Apple's new OS was hitting the news—which was all about lockscreen widgets. Glance, a Unicorn out of India, was announcing plans to bring *its* lockscreen platform to the US. The wave we foresaw almost seven years prior was happening. The value of the lock screen is unquestionable, and we had been innovating on it for years.

A David & Goliath Partnership

It was troubling to feel like your idea—the baby you've been nurturing for years—would get picked up by someone else with more resources to bring it to its full potential. (When iPhone released their update, even their font was the same as Vyng's.) That's when it occurred to us that Vyng has always been playing David to the major Goliath's of the industry. Perhaps aligning with a company with greater resources, who already has the OEM relationships we are seeking, would be a better game plan.

So, we got to work. Knowing the patents were our greatest asset, I emailed one hundred people closest to Vyng, from shareholders to advisors. I asked to speak with mergers and acquisitions experts that have sold large portfolios. After thirty intro offers, I spoke with fifteen of the best patent bankers and lawyers in the business. Within thirty days, and with a greater understanding of the landscape of patent M&A, I had offers for litigation, monetization, and partnership.

The Right Connections Change Everything

As fate would have it, an intro from our investor BAM Ventures (a VC founded by none other than Brian Lee from LegalZoom) led us to Fenwick Law Firm. A lawyer who participated on the intro call said he had a client who may be interested in our patents.

We were soon introduced to the CEO of Airfind, an extremely successful mobile ad and app company. The CEO, Aly, was an expert on lock screen video monetization. He basically looked at our app, which we had never monetized, and said, "You are sitting on a pile of gold." After two months of diligence, he introduced us to Fifth Partners where he was a limited partner. Fifth Partners is a $2 billion fund that was spearheading the creation of DigitalReef, a company building a premium media marketplace on mobile and CTV (Connected TV) across the Americas.

At the time, companies were looking for alternative ways to advertise outside of Facebook's and Google's ecosystems. Lyft, for example, was spinning up Lyft media to sell advertisements within their own cars. Meanwhile, telcos worldwide had long struggled to monetize their subscriber bases beyond selling SIM cards and data to third parties.

DigitalReef had a vision for using technological innovations to monetize mobile phone users through carrier partnerships. They could achieve this through a combination of acquisitions including mobile and CTV advertising networks, SIM card infrastructure technology, and partnerships with telcos that gave them a user base of over five hundred million.

DigitalReef wanted to own the entire user experience on mobile that is not in-app or in-browser. A significant portion of that user experience is lock screen-based (home screen, phone call, messaging, and notifications). Vyng happened to have knowledge, technology, and IP that is central to that strategy. By owning Vyng's assets, DigitalReef would be able to distribute Vyng's technology across its userbase in LATAM, monetize, and defend the IP from future competitors.

Was there a better partner in the world for Vyng?

The Perfect Union

Two and a half weeks from the initial intro, we got a letter of interest for acquisition. Sixty days later, we closed.

DigitalReef, which later merged with Gamers Club and became Siprocal, has since leveraged Vyng's patented technology that customizes the lock screen. This innovation has enabled Siprocal to connect global publishers and brands to its extensive footprint of more than 530 million registered devices, and more than three thousand active partnerships with carriers, manufacturers, publishers, and advertisers.

This ride of a lifetime culminated in finding the ideal partner to scale our technology and IP. From Tijuana road trips to coffee meetings across the world, we experienced the highs and lows of the roller coaster ride that defines the nature of entrepreneurship. The lessons we learned will last a lifetime, and we will continue to pursue the vision of visualizing communication across all mediums.

As one journey ends, another begins.

Mission: To the Moon

The following story is nothing short of a roller coaster. In my interview with Eric Salwan, a co-founder of Firefly Aerospace, a now public aerospace company with a market cap of $7 billion, you'll see how steadfast dedication to your vision can create miracles, even against the toughest odds.

My best friend from college, Christa, married her high school sweetheart, a guy named Tom Markusic. Tom became a rocket scientist, first working at NASA, then becoming one of the early SpaceX employees, running their McGregor test site. While visiting Tom at SpaceX, they were doing a rocket engine test. He sent me and a couple of his engineers to watch it from the field, and having never been to a rocket engine test before I asked, "Is this safe?"

They said, "Oh, yeah, we do it all the time."

The test started. It was amazing. It looked like a space shuttle taking off with giant, billowing clouds of white steam, the ground shaking…and then, *boom*, it *exploded* right in front of us! There was shrapnel flying all over the place. A big chunk of smoking metal landed probably twenty feet or thirty feet in front of us! That was my introduction to the world of rockets.

I knew the space industry was risky, but I also knew Tom was one of the few people that had what it took to do something extraordinary like start a space company and succeed. I was one of the first seed investors in Firefly before eventually coming to work at the company.

The capital required to do something like this is insane. Neither of us had ever tried to start a big company and raise big money. So, Tom took on business partners that assured him they'd manage the business side, including raising the money.

Once we made it to our Series A, a $30 million round, Paul Allen (co-founder of Microsoft) through his Vulcan Aerospace company put in $15 million, the other $15 million was a multinational deal coming out of the UK. Brexit happened. The pound crashed. That $15 million disappeared overnight. Without the remaining $15 million, we would run out of money and have to shut down the company.

The Sunday before our final week, after church, Tom, Christa, and I walked through Firefly in the dark, knelt, and started praying for strength and determination. We figured out that it costs $10,000 a day to pay 160 people minimum wage, which all the employees had agreed to in order to avoid layoffs. If Tom, Christa, me, Michael, and PJ—Tom's other co-founders—would each pay for a day, that would give us five days to figure out what to do.

On Wednesday, all the leadership team was sitting in the conference room working to get a loan. It was our final Hail Mary. It was not happening. We were all devastated. I realized tomorrow was my day to pay, so I said,

"I'll pay for tomorrow." Michael said to me, "Eric, you know, you're never going to get that money back."

I replied, "Michael, ten years from now, I don't want to be looking back and wondering if 10K would have made the difference." At that point, I only had $25,000 left in my bank account.

The next morning, on September 29th, 2016, we came in knowing we were shutting down Firefly and laying off 160 people. It was painful, with Tom crying, while employees were thanking him for the chance to do something that many had only ever dreamed of doing. But after laying everybody off, it turned into a giant party. The team wanted a picture, so we got everyone together and I took it.

Not long before, we had completed a successful full mission duty cycle engine test, which consists of running the rocket engine for the full duration of 206 seconds. On September 28, I put out a press release about the mission duty cycle. Tom thought I was crazy, saying, "You can't put out a press release when we're shutting down the company." But I saw that Elon was doing this big presentation about his Mars vision and thought since people can't invest in SpaceX, maybe they will see this press release and invest in Firefly.

I put the press release on my personal credit card with maximum exposure, then Firefly shut down. The team picture ended up on Twitter, and the engine test press release became a big story on a major engineering website.

With no one else left, Tom and I still went into the empty office every day to work. Leaving no stone unturned, we were contacting everyone who we thought could invest.

It's possible—and I don't know for sure—but it's possible that that picture of the team that we put on Twitter and article about the successful test is what Max saw when he got interested in Firefly.

Max Polyakov, a Ukrainian businessman, showed up at Firefly by having his team call the front desk and leave a voicemail for Tom. Max eventually bought up all our loans and foreclosed on them, forcing the company into bankruptcy. He then recapitalized and restarted Firefly, bringing back Tom as CEO.

Max, alone, would go on to fund the company for the next four years, putting over $200 million into Firefly. At the end of the four years, he gave up his green card and could no longer be involved with Firefly monetarily. We had around $20 million left in the bank, with a burn rate of about $6 to 10 million a month, depending how much we could cut back.

This is where the magic and the miracle showed up. I had spent years trying to get people interested in investing in Firefly, building up a network, and keeping people up to date on what we were up to. I gave my friend Mo, who I'd known since his days at JP Morgan, a tour early on and continued to nurture our friendship over the years.

During our Series A funding round, pursuing the bankers and professionals was a failing route, so I reached out to Mo asking if he knew anybody that might be interested. Mo called his friend, Ryan, saying, "I told you to invest in SpaceX and you didn't. I told you to invest in

Relativity and you didn't. Now I'm telling you to invest in Firefly." Ryan became our Series A lead investor, setting the valuation at a billion dollars and writing a multimillion-dollar check.

Another friend of mine was an early crypto guy, David. Tom met David and could tell he wasn't going to invest—the minimal check size was outside his comfort level. That didn't bother me though. I knew David was a solid guy, loved the space industry, and was excited about Firefly. I gave him the full VIP tour, including an amazing rocket engine test (that didn't blow up). While David didn't invest personally, he did connect me with a few of his friends in the crypto space, including Jed McCaleb, the founder of Ripple and Stellar cryptocurrencies. Tom and Jed hit it off, but Max was unconvinced. He thought Jed was a "fake billionaire." I finally got Max to do a call with him. Jed ended up being the biggest investor in the round and also significantly bought down Max's position in a separate transaction.

I've been on a spiritual path for many years. I believe being open to the opportunities Spirit shows you and remaining in flow with what is and what could be can create non-linear results you can't "think" your way to. You never know where a "chance" meeting will lead.

We had less than thirty days of runway left when we closed the Series A. We would have gone bankrupt, again. The only reason we didn't was because my friends called up their friends and told them to invest in Firefly. Fast forward to today, it's still a challenge raising money for a space company. But the series D lead investor was brought in by Ryan, our series A lead investor. All told, my friends and their network and the extended network of the people they've brought in have invested over $280 million in Firefly.

And then on March 2, 2025, we landed on the Moon.

The true end of a journey is not dictated by external setbacks but by the decision to keep going or not. Despite losing critical funding, shutting down operations, and facing near-impossible odds, the persistence of Eric and the team, along with the relentless drive to find new opportunities, ultimately revived Firefly and led to its billion-dollar IPO. Eric's story exemplifies that being an entrepreneur means taking charge of your destiny. At critical junctions, Eric chose to keep pushing forward. His resilience, resourcefulness, and unwavering belief in the possibility of Firefly's success helped keep it alive to eventually make good on its proposed vision for aerospace technology.

Make It Real: "Nothing Dies Until You Say So"

Key Takeaways

- The only real ending is the one you accept. There will be times when it seems like you don't have options, but if you're in that moment, I invite you to keep pushing—you'll be glad you did.
- Your biggest assets might not be what you expect. Sometimes, success isn't about scaling your business alone but about aligning with the right players who can.

- Relentless outreach: your community and network are one email away.

Workbook Exercise: The "Last Bullet" Challenge

Inspired by Eric Salwan's quote, this exercise helps you push past obstacles when you feel like giving up.

1. Define the battle: What's the challenge you're facing?
2. List every "bullet" you have left: What strategies, contacts, skills, or resources haven't you fully leveraged?
3. Throw the gun: If traditional strategies aren't working, what's a completely different approach you haven't tried?
4. Go hand-to-hand: If you had to make something work without any funding, support, or perfect conditions, what would you do?

AI Prompt: "I'm thinking about giving up on [insert idea/project] because [brief reason]. Help me assess whether there's still potential—or if it's time to pivot or let it go. Be honest."

No battle is over until you decide it is. What's your next move?

PART
2
(YOUR TURN)

DISCOVER YOUR BIG IDEA

"In all entrepreneurs, there's a moment of vision, the moment of desire, where you realize this is what I want to do. This is what I need to do."

—Edward Shenderovich (founder of Knotel, $1.3 billion peak value)

Every idea has the potential to be the seed that starts something amazing. Every company that you know of, from Airbnb to Slack to Netflix…all of them started with a single idea. Someone was sitting down one day with their version of a "Wouldn't it be cool if…?" statement.

My interview with Fred Krueger, an entrepreneur whose innovations span industries, was a wild masterclass in coming up with great ideas. His journey with Matisse is a robust story that hits a few key ideas in *High Five Energy*.

151

I was in Northern India on a trip with my first wife, my brother, and his wife. We were talking about life when I mentioned wanting to exit finance and maybe create a company. I asked my brother if he had any ideas, and he said, "I think 3D software is going to be a huge industry."

I said, "Oh! 3D software—medical software?"

He confirmed, "Yeah, medical 3D software."

That sounded intriguing to me. I had some context in 3D technology because Jim Clark, who started Silicon Graphics, had been a professor of mine at Stanford. With my limited understanding of 3D graphics, I felt the idea had merit. My brother, a computer science guy working in Singapore at the time, also had some knowledge of the state of 3D rendering and software. This was about thirty years ago, so the field was still in its early stages. We agreed over beers in India to start the company.

We later moved to North Carolina, where we were originally from, and we started building the company. We decided to buy a Silicon Graphics machine to develop the 3D software, even though we had no idea what we were doing. When we approached Silicon Graphics to buy the machine, they asked us for a business plan. I was baffled. "We're buying the machine," I said. "Why do you need a business plan?" They needed to ensure they weren't selling it to just anyone, which I thought was ridiculous—having to pitch a business plan just to buy a computer. But my brother was adamant in thinking Silicon Graphics was the future.

I went to a bookstore—Windows 3.0 had just come out. I said, "You know, Richard, I see all these books on

Windows 3.0. And you're telling me Silicon Graphics is the future? Uh, I don't think so. We need to do something on Windows 3.0. Do you know anything about it?"

He goes, "No, I don't."

"Well, we're about to learn." I bought books, technical manuals, developer guides, OLE 2.0, and a Borland C compiler for Windows. The next day we embarked on our Windows project. We still had no idea what we were going to do. So, I asked him what he wanted to build.

He said, "Well, I made this paint program at IBM a while ago." I asked to see it, and he showed me the demo video.

I thought, *This is great. Let's put that thing on Windows.*

That was it. That was the beginning. There was no more thought beyond the understanding that Windows is taking off, and they don't seem to have a paint program, so we are going to be the ones to build it. It took us a full year to go from day one to having shrink-wrapped software. Back then, you couldn't just update and fix bugs all the time like you can now. You had to create a golden master—a version without bugs. It turned out to be really good timing.

There were a few very primitive games like Microsoft Olympics, where you could run around a track or throw a javelin. Then we created our tool for Windows that allowed you to paint with charcoal, watercolors, and the like. And people just loved it. They said, "Oh my God, I can become like Matisse." The program hit just exactly right; we had product market fit. It lasted for a good year and a half, just that one product without any changes and we continued selling it.

And really, that's the thing about being a developer or entrepreneur: you never know if you're going to hit. But you ultimately have to trust your gut and take your shot—despite what the ethos is focusing on.

After our success with Matisse, we decided to create another version of it. Matisse itself was this huge commercial hit, right? We sold millions of dollars of this software, bundled in with all these scanners…and then we basically said, "Okay, now we've got to build the more adult version." We built this other product called xRes, which had all these problems, but it was a very ambitious project. And in a way, that was a mistake because we were positioning ourselves to compete with Photoshop. The big problem with Photoshop at the time, we're talking 1993, was Photoshop couldn't handle big images. There was prepress they needed to use to handle images in gigabytes, which were ultimately problematic. And you just couldn't do it without having tons and tons of memory, costing hundreds of thousands of dollars…and Photoshop couldn't handle it very well. Now we would not think of them as big images, but at the time, things were different. So, xRes was trying to solve that problem by being able to handle super high-resolution images.

It demoed really well. But, from a practical point of view, like LivePicture (another competitor at the time), it wasn't super practical for the prepress world where we intended it for, and which we didn't really know. So, while that endeavor did not do well, I count it toward our successes too, because that is ultimately what enabled us to sell the company to Macromedia—because xRes is what they wanted. They came to us, and they said, "Okay, we'll offer you $10 million for your company."

And I said, "Listen, I'm making over a million dollars a year right now in this company. Why would I sell it for $10 million? I'm selling it at 10 P/E. I'm not going to do that. That's crazy."

They then asked, "What do you propose?"

And I said, "$20 million."

And they were like, "Yeah, we can't pay $20 million."

I essentially said, "Well, great. Nice knowing you. See you later." My brother almost had a heart attack! Asking why didn't I take the $10 million?

Then they came back to the table, and they offered $15 million. I said, "Done deal." We sold the company for $15 million in Macromedia stock. Macromedia stock doubled. Which meant by the time we finished selling, it was worth $30 million. This is 1995, not a lot of people are selling their companies for $30 million back then.

There are layers in this story that hit archetypal stages in the entrepreneurial journey. Leaving or refusing a stable job is *typically* a first step in starting something yourself. Despite knowing little about the 3D software space, Fred dives in and embarks on a new adventure. He pivots to Windows and creates a paint program, emphasizing that taking risks and trusting your instincts are important skills for any entrepreneur. What takes Fred across the finish line, and enables him to ultimately sell his company, is his capacity to work reality in his favor.

The negotiation process with Macromedia highlights the importance of understanding and reframing value, even when xRes failed to meet its intended purpose, Fred viewed it as a stepping stone rather than a setback, making it the clinch point that led to the sale of Fauve Software to Macromedia. Fred's story shows how identifying a vision, inspired by a moment of insight, can fuel the development of your business.

Make It Real: Your "Discover Your Big Idea" Challenge

How can you think of *your* big idea? Try this exercise.

1. For the next five days, write down three ideas per day.
   - "Wouldn't it be cool if _____?"
     - Wouldn't it be cool if I could share a taxi?
     - Wouldn't it be cool if I controlled the content on my friend's phone call?
2. After five days, *rank them* on a spreadsheet in order of the best idea to the worst.
   a. Factors can include estimated cost, time, and, most importantly, your excitement level.
   b. There is a chance—a good chance—that one of those ideas is worth pursuing or at least exploring further.
3. If nothing stands out as worth pursuing, do the exercise again.

AI Prompt: "Here are three interests or obsessions I keep coming back to: [insert them]. Help me identify a business or product idea that connects them—something that would feel meaningful and exciting to build."

Try to focus on things that could significantly affect *your* life and the people around you. Most great ideas were inspired by something personal to the person who came up with it. When you start viewing the world as malleable, as something you can shape—"Wouldn't it be cool if...?"—in time, will lead you to your big idea.

Inspiration from Fred:

For Fred, his list of "Wouldn't be cool if...?" ideas is a masterclass in entrepreneurial creativity, reshaping many different industries.

Wouldn't it be cool if...

1. ...artists could digitally paint and edit images with software built just for them? (Fauve Software acquired by Macromedia)
2. ...data analysis tools automatically uncovered meaningful patterns from massive datasets? (RandomNoise acquired by Vignette)
3. ...playing simple online games could lead to real prizes and rewards? (iWin acquired by Vivendi)
4. ...digital ad placements were easy, targeted, and scalable for advertisers? (TrafficMarketplace acquired by Vivendi)
5. ...anyone could quickly build their own personalized social network? (TagWorld acquired by Viacom)

6. ...mobile advertising could precisely target users in real-time? (Gradient X acquired by Singtel)
7. ...digital ads could be efficiently distributed world-wide from a unified platform? (Adconion acquired by Singtel)
8. ...brands could effortlessly optimize their marketing spend and reach through machine learning? (Five Delta acquired by SRAX)
9. ...managing internet domain names was simplified and more accessible? (MMX acquired by GoDaddy)
10. ...cryptocurrency wallets were simple enough for anyone to securely transact with ease? (Lynx acquired by Metal Pay)

Yes, that's ten total exits valued at over $500 million.

What's your big idea?

Want to watch the full interview with Fred Kreuger?
Visit: www.jeffreychernick.com

DO WHAT YOU LOVE

> "I never had a master plan. It was a series of right moves
> along a very long journey, fueled by my first and most
> fundamental goal: to make a living doing what we love
> without working for somebody else. That was the goal."
>
> —Lynda Weinman, co-founder of Lynda.com ($1.5 billion exit)

There is an amazing video on YouTube by philosopher Alan Watts called "What If Money Was No Object?"

He poses the question, "What would you like to do if money were no object? How would you really enjoy spending your life?" By using the parameters of infinite capital, it creates a field of possibility. In this hypothetical situation, you are no longer limited by preconceived constraints that narrow your perception of what you can create for yourself. You can imagine a world where you follow your true passions.

There's an Audience for Your Passion

Watts's basic premise (and I clearly agree) is that to lead a fulfilled life, it's better to do what you love than what you assume is "appropriate." He also reveals that with the amount of people in the world, you are sure to find (or create) a market for what you love. Among the eight billion people on Earth—each with their different likes, interests, hobbies, perspectives, desires, needs, and wants—someone is bound to share similar interests as you.

For example, if you love creating art and you are passionate and dedicated, simply by a measure of how many people there are on the planet, we can assume there will be enough of them who will recognize your artistry and support your work. If you love numbers and thrill at the idea of organizing them, perhaps explore being an accountant. If you love coming up with ideas, be an entrepreneur…

Overcoming Societal Pressures

It's not an easy concept to wrap your mind around at first. Societal constructs, our parents, even our peers can contribute to the idea that "path X" is the *right* or *wrong* path for you. These influences create pressure to pursue a particular path that is proposed as a *sure thing*. Yet, every successful and happy person I know chose to follow their joy into a professional career. Moreover, with advancements in AI and a shifting political landscape, careers typically viewed as "sure things" are no longer as stable as they once were.

You can, of course, find success in doing things that don't make you happy…but then what is the measure we use to define "success?" We are holistic beings, and more and more studies reveal that once basic needs are met, additional money doesn't make you happier.

It's Really That Simple

Life is too short *not* to do what you love. If you can focus inward long enough to discover what you love to do—that thing that keeps you up at night because you are excited and engaged—do that! You can most likely create a career out of it. And there are enough people in the world that someone, many someones, are bound to align with your vision.

Do What You Love: It Pays Off in the End

The following story is from my interview with Jack Dangermond, co-founder and current president of Esri (Environmental Systems Research Institute), a global leader in geographic information system (GIS) technology and digital mapping. Jack's passion for geography and environmental science powers Esri's impact, which extends beyond software. It has fundamentally changed how we understand and interact with the world. Esri has grown to become a dominant force in GIS software, generating over $2 billion dollars in annual revenue, with no outside capital raised.

It was in May of 1969. Laura and I were still at Harvard, working in a lab for computer mapping and spatial analysis. That is the place where mapping with a computer was first invented.

These classes were taught by some pretty amazing people. John Kenneth Galbraith, Ed Wilson, and B. F. Skinner were there. It was a really amazing and enlightening time for us.

Upon finishing our work at the lab and completing our degrees, on a Saturday afternoon in May, we decided to sit around—no concrete outcomes to be had—and ask the question: What should we do next?

Silent Spring by Rachel Carson (published in 1962, is a groundbreaking environmental science book that exposed the devastating effects of chemical pesticides on ecosystems) had come out and deeply inspired me.

We had nice offers to stay there at Harvard and other offers from Berkeley and Minnesota. But we sought to figure out what we really *wanted* to do. While it's pretty abstract, we thought first: rational behavior. At the time, Harvard was full of protests about the Vietnam War and civil rights and other issues.

People were going to the right, going to the left. It didn't interest us. What did interest us was rational systems thinking and the use of computers to address environmental challenges, urban design, and urban planning challenges. So, we didn't actually make a decision to start a business, we made a decision to ground ourselves in rational thinking. That was the foundation of our life's work.

The science of the world is all built on geography, it's everything. Everything is organized by geography, all cultural geography, sociology, economics, the natural world, biology, geology, climatology, all the ologies really come together under geography. So geography, to me, is everything. Having a career in geography opened up the world to me. By focusing on one thing, I was granted access to everything. I could look at studying the oceans. We have; I spent millions on ocean GIS. Or look at biodiversity geography, which we did with my good friend before he passed away, Ed Wilson. Or I could go in the direction of city planning, or I could go in the direction of landscape planning, and I find all of it so fun.

This is hard to believe, but we have about ten million customers who use our tools, and they are organized into 680,000 organizations. One organization is the USGS. When I visit them, they show me the vast expanse of their work: fish and game, Fish and Wildlife Service, topographic mapping, the remote sensing of lands. It's incredibly diverse.

Essentially, I have this highly focused life of building tools that help our users do their work better. We do that generically, not very focused. Then our customers take those tools, and they build out refined applications, which are quite sophisticated in their particular domain.

I push for making things interrelated using our common platform. Over time, this approach has brought our customers together in ways that reveal the deep interconnections between industries. Take climate change, for example—it's driven by rising carbon levels, which stem from oil and coal extraction, fueled by our need for energy. That energy demand powers everything from cars to businesses like FedEx and UPS. And it doesn't stop there—housing, economic equity, infrastructure invest-ments, and taxation are all part of the same intercon-nected system.

By focusing on one thing—developing generic tools that apply to everything—I'm able to work across indus-tries while staying true to a singular mission. In the end, everything is related, and the right tools help us see and act on those connections.

Our number one purpose is to serve our users. First through services and later with products. We spend about a third of our revenue on advancing our product, always in service to the user. Our second purpose is to cultivate a culture that supports our employees, helping them realize their life's work. That's a big goal here. From competitive pay to comprehensive healthcare, we provide strong sup-port, sharing 20 percent of our profits with employees. We take living a purposeful life seriously, even if we don't always talk about it.

Today, our partner revenue—generated through our software's integration—stands between $35 and $40 billion, positioning us within a much larger geospatial business ecosystem.

It's not about selling it, getting rich quick, or arriving at the big exit strategy young kids are taught to pursue. That's a different kind of interest. For me, the reward is doing the work on everything, tackling a wide range of challenges that I find both interesting and fulfilling. I think about having ten million users working on complex issues around the world. They're working on everything.

Jack's story illustrates how doing what you love can lead to both fulfillment and impact. He and his wife, Laura, pursued a career rooted in personal passion for rational, information-driven work that would shape environmental and land-use decisions around the world. By focusing on geography, a subject he deeply loved, Jack unlocked opportunities across industries. His passion-driven approach led to immense personal satisfaction, but also to a thriving business that supports the satisfaction of their employees as well. The creation of tools that empower millions to solve global challenges is an inspiring story.

Make It Real: Your "Do What You Love" Challenge

Choosing meaningful work doesn't limit you, it expands what is possible.

Key Takeaways

- The most fulfilling careers are built around what you truly enjoy.
- There is an audience for nearly every passion; your unique interests can align with market demand.
- Societal expectations and external pressures often push people toward "safe" choices, but long-term success is built on alignment between work and joy.

Your Action Plan: Courage to Pursue What You Love

- List five things you love doing (the things that excite you, that you lose track of time doing).

- Do any of your ideas from "Discover Your Big Idea" align with what you love?
- If yes, identify potential markets:
  - Who might be interested in what you love to do?
  - Who could benefit from it?

AI Prompt: "I love doing [insert activity or topic], and I lose track of time when I [insert experience]. Help me brainstorm ways this could become a business, offering, or product that adds value to others."

TALK ABOUT IT!

I've come across countless entrepreneurs who are hesitant to share information about their startup. They shy away from telling anybody about their vision for fear of others "stealing their idea." Here's the thing: it's all about implementation. Choosing to steal your idea means spending the next three to five years on making it a reality, and dedicating time and resources to its inception. While I am sure there are exceptions, it's more likely than not that no one is taking your baby—or at minimum following through.

The Value in Talking About It

My sister is a pediatric emergency room doctor in Manhattan, NY. Having only heard stories, I was curious about the realities of her profession. A few years after college, I shadowed her for one night to get an idea of what a typical overnight looked like. I got to see first-hand what it was like to be a doctor. It was incredible. And at times surprisingly boring. Other moments were exhausting. I got a front row seat to the work culture, interactions with patients, difficult hours, and the rewarding nature of serving others in need.

I repeated this experience with a friend of mine who had a sales job and again with another friend who did tech support.

Wouldn't It Be Cool If...

One of my ideas was called Jampling. The name was derived from my exploration in *sampling* various *jobs*.

As a young student, I wished there was a way to experience a job before choosing a career path. Teachers ask kids what they want to be when they grow up, and when you're a kid, you have no idea what that actually entails. In college, many students choose their profession without really knowing what it's like to wake up at 6:00 AM and go to an investment bank in a suit, six days a week. Some people love it, some people hate it.... But wouldn't it be cool if you could experience that early? Try before you buy.

Testing The Market: Jampling

Jampling was a company that would partner with large employers looking to hire top, post-graduate talent. We would partner with universities and create a matching program that could allow students to sample jobs for a certain period of hours in a given school year.

With only a simple idea—no website, sales deck, or marketing material—I reached out to HR managers at various companies to get real feedback on the viability of my idea.

Circumventing the usual biases around ethnicity, gender, and age is often accomplished by picking up the phone. The HR representatives (who were pretty easy to get a hold of) received the idea positively.

Lessons from Talking About It

Even with positive feedback, I found there was a lot of red tape in terms of safety and data security. Especially in today's age, those security concerns are that much greater. But I would not have learned that unless I took the first steps, which in this case was speaking to the target market. Had I not shared Jampling with the very people who could potentially steal it, I never would have discovered the nuances that ultimately deterred me from pursuing it.

For all you readers out there, I recently gave up the website, Jampling.com, so you're more than welcome to pursue it.

So talk about it. Share your ideas with those around you, seek opinions, and get creative. If the book thus far has failed to articulate it enough, feedback is *essential* to creating the best version of something.

The following story is from my interview with Eytan Elbaz, an entrepreneur and investor best known for co-founding Applied Semantics and Scopely, a mobile gaming startup ($5 billion exit). We originally met at an investor conference when he came up to me and said, "Aren't you the drummer from Story of the Running Wolf?" After confirming I was, he said, "Why are you wearing a suit?" Turns out he was a fan of my band, and we quickly became friends. In his story, we'll learn how *talking about it* landed him his first angel check.

The biggest leap I took was quitting my job for that first startup. I was twenty-five years old. I was working for a big company, AMD, and I had just gotten a raise to $85,000 a year. They also paid for my four-door Volvo and an alphanumeric page. I wore a suit every day, which at the time, felt really cool to me. It took me three years to get to this place where I felt good and secure, and I looked like I had an important job.

At the same time, it was 1998, and I couldn't help but be mesmerized by what was happening in the stock market for internet companies. My brother, a couple other guys, and I would spend our evenings talking about all sorts of startup ideas and brainstorming about what we can do in this new economy.

We landed on an idea to build an open-source Yahoo-like directory to compete with Yahoo.com. This was called Oingo and would ultimately become Applied Semantics. We wrote a business plan, and I started talking to everybody about what we wanted to build.

We grew up quite middle-class. When we decided to start a company, there was no clear person to go to and ask for money. We asked my grandmother's cousin's husband because we knew him to be successful. We thought to ask my childhood friend's father because he had sold a dental practice and figured he might have some investment capital. Neither invested. We were multiple steps away from anybody who had any real capital to invest. There was no one in our immediate circle who could write a hundred-thousand-dollar check.

So we started generally telling everybody what it was that we were doing. You never know who you might be speaking to—whether they might know somebody who could be an investor—or an employee or a customer. I would softly put the company out there frequently in conversation, and if they latch on to it, then I'd continue talking about it to see if they could play one of those three roles.

It's important to be self-aware when talking to everybody about what you're building. It's a fine line: You don't want to pester people who do not have the ability or the interest in your company, but you don't want to miss out on the opportunity of building a productive relationship. Put it out there and see if they could be one of those three things, an employee, an investor, or a customer. If there's a little something there, you can keep talking to them about it. If there's not, you move on like a normal human being, and you don't keep talking about your startup.

Our first $500,000 check came from one of my customers at AMD, who had been talking about a startup PC business they were looking to build. During our meeting, which took place while I was with my previous employer, I said, "I have this other business I'm working on. It's an internet software business." And they said they were interested. So, I said, "How about we do this? I'd like to come back here after work hours, bring my co-founder, and we'll talk about this in a more meaningful way." We came back thirty-six hours later and told them what we were doing.

The morning after that, they called me back and said they were prepared to fund us at the terms we put forth the previous night. Seven days later, we had a term sheet.

Compared to what other internet companies were raising at the time, it wasn't a great deal of money. We'd only be able to afford to pay me $40,000 a year, no health benefits or supplemental car payments. I had been working at this increased salary at AMD for just ninety days and had to take a 60 percent comp cut to go and do all of this.

This risk was all amplified by the likelihood that it's at least a multi-year commitment.

It was a big fork in the road for me, but I took the riskier path and quit my job about thirty days after hearing the PC guys were willing to fund us. Fortunately, it worked out.

When asked if I was afraid to talk about my business ideas to people, I like to say that most ideas are commodities. There are very few ideas that are rare or unique. What is rare or unique is your personal passion and personal take or execution of the idea. It's very unlikely the person you're talking to is going to be as excited about that idea as you are. If there is some secret sauce, you might choose to hold that piece back. But besides that, get out there and talk about your idea so that you can build yourself a variety of opportunities. Just do it in a thoughtful and deliberate way.

After five years and eight pivots, Google acquired Eytan's company, Applied Semantics, for $102 million. Following the acquisition, the team's contextual advertising technology became foundational to Google's ad products—most notably powering the launch of Google AdSense. When Google last published AdSense revenues, they were over $30 billion annually and are believed to be substantially higher than that today.

Eytan's story reinforces the transformative power of sharing your ideas. It's also important to note that once he saw real possibilities from his then client, he didn't get into the details of it on company time. But he also didn't shy away from the risk of bringing it up in the first place. His story illustrates how talking about your vision in an intentional, respectful way can lead to connections, insights, breakthroughs and even a check that might have otherwise been missed. And again, with every entrepreneur's story, we see over and over how taking risks—whether to speak to someone or quit your stable job—is a major part of turning ideas into reality.

Make It Real: Your "Talk About It!" Challenge

Ideas aren't enough—execution is everything.

Key Takeaways

- Execution over ideas: your idea alone isn't enough; what matters is how you bring it to life. Most people won't steal your idea because success requires years of commitment and execution.
- Identify roadblocks before you invest years of effort.
- Conversations open doors. Talking about your idea helps you refine it, gain feedback, and connect with potential investors, collaborators, or customers.
- Share with intention. Be strategic about who you talk to and how you present your idea. Gauge interest, listen to feedback, and adapt.

Put It into Practice: Talk About It!

Now that we've aligned one of your ideas with what you love:

- Craft your pitch. In three to five sentences, describe your idea. Keep it simple, compelling, and clear.
- Choose three individuals you can share this idea with: someone in your industry, someone outside of it, and a potential user/customer.
- Ask for feedback. Engage in a short conversation with each person. Tell them it's your friend's idea—that way, people are more likely to be *brutally* honest.
  - What were their first impressions? What questions did they ask? Did their reactions shift your thinking in any way?
- Reflect and refine: What did you learn? Did their feedback spark new ideas, reveal blind spots, or confirm your direction?

AI Prompt: "I have an idea for [insert what you're building]. Help me write a short, confident way to explain it out loud—like I was telling a friend or mentor for the first time."

Want to watch the full interview with Eytan Elbaz?
Visit: www.jeffreychernick.com

ENROLL OTHERS IN YOUR VISION

Enrollment is a powerful tool for bringing ideas to life, whether you're building a business, launching a project, or creating anything in life. Enrollment doesn't just mean recruitment. It's a multidimensional acquisition of someone to adopt your vision as their own. It's a term describing the process of getting someone invested and inspired by what you are creating. They, in turn, are motivated to either work for you, give you funds, connect you with advisors, or offer support in various ways.

The Secret Sauce Is You

Many people think that enrollment is best achieved by proving that the nuts and bolts of the product or idea are sound and viable. However, much of what investors are banking on is *you*. Yes, of course, you need to have the product details up to snuff to secure funding and support, but the real bulk of what makes someone offer their time, capital, and resources is their faith and excitement about the people involved with the project. No one can predict the challenges and roadblocks along the journey. Investors seek out people who can weather the storm and find creative solutions.

Enrolling Your Team

Not only do you need to enroll people outside of your company for various needs, but enrolling your team is key to the success or failure of a company, as well. As a leader, you need to create a team that's fully engaged in your vision, so their decisions and efforts reflect a true sense of ownership of what becomes your shared vision. That is true enrollment.

When I founded RideAmigos, we needed a CTO to build the platform. Evan and I were introduced to Ben through Indiana University's alumni network. Ben loved the company's mission and agreed to work nights and weekends for 20 percent of the company. With the mission of RideAmigos now his vision too, Ben became a true partner, leading the company's technology growth over the next sixteen years. Not only does RideAmigos support Ben's family, but we've grown to support twenty-five other families as well.

At Vyng, Paul and I needed a CTO that understood what we were after. The person we wanted already had a job at Paul's last company. So what did we do? We enrolled Art to work nights and weekends for equity. After our first venture round, we had enough money so Art could quit his other job, devoting his time to Vyng—*his* vision.

The Dream Team

The most successful companies are the organizations in which the team members are not working to fulfill somebody else's interests but collectively working to fulfill the interests of a shared vision. That's why company culture is so important. If you can create a culture of shared values, predicated on fulfilling people's highest potential, mountains are moved. That's when people are willing to stay up nights and weekends to work on projects. Not just because they were paid overtime, but because they believed in something that's bigger than just one person's vision.

This story comes from my interview with Jim Armstrong, a venture capitalist who, well before investing in Vyng, backed PayPal in its early days, helping to develop the company until its $1.8 billion acquisition by eBay. Over his career, Jim Armstrong has generated $750 million in returns for his venture funds.

This is right before we became Clearstone and we were considered top one to three venture funds in the new industry called "the internet." Bill Trenchard called me and said, "You need to take a look at these guys. Peter and Max."

Bill was an entrepreneur I backed a year or two out of graduating Cornell. We had a company we built in the online productivity space, and Microsoft bought it. It was real quick, a year-round trip. He moved out west and became a VC himself at First Round capital.

And I'll say this: the reasons I invested were first, Max. He developed a really neat piece of software that had a neat quirk to it. Without going into details, it had something differentiated about the way it processed payments, particularly, the way it could propagate faster, along with security features. Those turned out to be the key elements in the whole operation, quite frankly.

The second reason was Peter. He was really smart and had a clear grasp of the industry. I think he was a currency trader before that, as I recall. He was brilliant.

So, we invested $5 million for 20 percent of the company and led the early round. Nokia Ventures had put some money in as a strategic because it was originally designed for an early smartphone called the Palm Pilot or Palm Treo; we pivoted later, but this was seven to eight years before the iPhone.

But, again, I invested because they demonstrated great knowledge, and Max's technology was special. Though it hadn't even launched yet, we had a few pilots where people were beaming money around on phones, which showcased the trick: the software beamed *with* the money. So normally you have a user one problem. When adopting new technology someone would say for example, "Oh, I don't have this product 'PayPal' by this company 'Confinity.'" That's alright. The software for the product beams with the money. So, there was no user one problem. Max developed that.

Sometime after we launched, we pivoted to email because phones were too small of a user base. It surprised us and shocked us that it took off on eBay. eBay had their own product at the time called Billpoint, and they were trying to kill us. And then X.com—the first "X.com,"

Elon loves that name—was an online mutual fund that also did some payments. They were right next door to PayPal on University Avenue. They used to accuse each other of stealing their screenshots out of dumpster bins. Again, this is a long time ago…

But when it came down to the merger, after our first couple of board meetings post pivot, I remember looking at the board deck and I had never seen user growth like that. You could just tell this was going to be major. And I'll never forget, Peter came to me afterwards so apologetic, saying, "I'm so sorry to the board"—which was just me and Nokia Ventures—"that we have no revenue model."

And I quickly jumped in, "Don't worry, alright? You're moving money. There's a revenue model embedded."

Peter said, "I want to merge with X because they have a better management team." And it was funny, Peter and I were the exact opposite of most VC/entrepreneur dynamics. The entrepreneur typically says, "I want to run the company," while the VC says, "No, we need to bring someone in." We were the opposite. Peter kept insisting he was not the right person to run the company. I'd meet some of the people he wanted to replace him, and I'd say, "You're about forty IQ points higher, and you make better decisions." It was also obvious even then that he made great hiring decisions. We would continue to have this debate all the way up to the IPO. This is jumping ahead in the story, but I remember the night before the IPO, he called me and said, "We got to find a CEO for this company."

I said, "Peter, we're going public tomorrow! You're the CEO!"

But back to the merger, Peter insisted saying, "I want you to meet X, and I've kind of told him that we're going to merge." I informed him that it was important to run that by the board. Once we got into it, he said X wanted an eighty/twenty deal, which he thought was good—what? I found that shocking. Now, we had no revenue, and they had revenue, but we had the product. So, Elon, the founder of X, and I sat down at Il Fornaio in Palo Alto. Peter and I agreed that I was going to go negotiate this deal. It was a long conversation where we talked about a lot of things.

It was obvious that Elon was the brightest bulb on their side. They had an industry CEO who was a good guy, but he wasn't Elon. Peter was right, Elon and team did offer a lot of value, but I wasn't convinced we couldn't bring in value through other means. Eventually I just said, "Let's do fifty/fifty." Elon put his hand across the table, and we shook on it.

That was how we structured a merger of equals—something I wasn't entirely happy about at the time, as I thought we had everything teed up for success. But in hindsight, it was the right move, as Peter's instincts about X's team being the right partner proved correct.

PayPal is still PayPal today. Though eBay gets a lot of credit for that.

eBay bought it the night before the lockup came off, almost six months after the IPO for I think a billion

> eight. So, it was a good return, and it's since gone on to become a really successful company.

What sticks out the most about the experience is getting to work with really great people. And that was why I invested.

Jim invested in PayPal[2] not just because of Max's innovative technology, but because both Max and Peter demonstrated deep industry knowledge, the ability to pivot when necessary, and the ability to execute on their vision. Even before the product had fully launched, their competence and vision made them worth betting on. PayPal's trajectory, its pivot to email payments, its unexpected success on eBay, its partnership with X.com, and its eventual acquisition was a direct result of that special team and their ability to enroll the right people along for the ride.

Make It Real: Your "Enrollment" Challenge

Investors don't just look for the best product; they look for the best people who can adapt, execute, and build something enduring.

Key Takeaways

- Enrollment is not recruitment; it's about inspiring others to adopt *your* vision as *their own*.

---

[2] **Fun Fact:** The group of early PayPal leaders would later become known as the "PayPal Mafia," a legendary network of founders and investors who went on to create some of the most successful tech companies of the next two decades, including Tesla, Affirm, LinkedIn, Yelp, and Palantir. This reinforces the value in enrolling the right team.

- Investors back people as much as (or more than) they back products.
- True enrollment creates a shared vision within a company, leading to greater ownership and commitment.

Enrollment Challenge: Win Someone Over

Instead of just writing a pitch, put your enrollment skills to the test in a live interaction.

Step 1: Choose a Real Opportunity

Let's build the support for your new endeavor. It could be:

- Convincing a friend or colleague to join your project.
- Getting someone to try your new product, service, or experience (to get feedback).
- Pitching an investor.

Step 2: Prepare Your Approach

- Frame the vision. What are you creating, and why does it matter?
- Find the hook. Why would this person care? What excites or motivates *them*?
- Make it personal. Show them how they fit into the vision and what's in it for them.
- Be open to feedback. Enrollment isn't just pitching; it's co-creating. Be ready to adjust based on their reactions.

Step 3: Execute and Reflect

- Have the conversation. See if you can genuinely inspire and enroll them.

- Did they get excited? Were they hesitant? What worked, and what didn't?
- If they didn't commit, why not? Adjust your approach and try again with someone else.

AI Prompt: "Help me write a short, powerful vision statement for my [business or project]. It should feel exciting, clear, and like something people would want to get behind. Now rework it for [a potential co-founder, early hire, or investor.]"

Enrollment is a skill that strengthens with repetition. Keep practicing with different people in different situations. Over time, you'll refine your ability to inspire and rally people around your vision.

Want to watch the full interview with Jim Armstrong?
Visit: www.jeffreychernick.com

ASK FOR ADVICE

When you have an opportunity to meet someone who you admire, or perhaps someone who is further down a path you'd like to emulate, it's good practice to just ask them for advice.

Most likely they have been in your shoes. They've started low on the totem pole. They've been intimidated. They've both failed and succeeded. Deep down they understand what it's like to be young, inexperienced, or just starting out.

Be Honest and Open

When given the opportunity to connect, be honest and open. If you're feeling nervous, say, "I'm feeling nervous." If you're feeling intimidated, call it out. By acknowledging your feelings in real-time, out loud, it immediately alleviates a huge chunk of tension and also gives the person you're meeting with an opportunity to make you feel better. I know it's easier said than done, but the truth is authenticity is so important in cultivating a real connection with someone. Asking for advice opens the door, and being authentic is the way through it.

Do Your Research

Also, make sure to do your research on the person's background. That way you can ask meaningful and relevant questions. People often appreciate an opportunity to share about themselves. Demonstrating that you've taken the time to understand their work shows respect and initiative, making it more likely they'll engage with you seriously. Thoughtful questions can also lead to deeper, more insightful conversations, nurturing a genuine connection.

Get Curious About Them

"If you were in my shoes, how would you go about doing X?" Ask specific questions about how they operate and how they got to where they are. Not only could it be great advice, but you might have a great time listening.

As people start to create a real connection with you, they will be more inclined to support what you're up to and even connect you to their network.

In my interview with Jeff Hoffman, he tells a great story about how asking for advice was the key to breaking into a new industry.

Everybody wants to be successful just until they find out what it takes. The stuff I did, anybody could do. However, you have to be willing to do the work. When I started thinking about producing a concert, I was busy with my day job, so every night I was researching the industry. I was reading everything I could that Google had to offer about how to produce a concert.

Then I discovered in all that research that the concert industry, like every industry, has its own publication. It's a magazine called *Pollstar*. Never heard of it in my life. I subscribed to it, and I immediately noticed something at the end of every article: a byline.

Every time I read an article, I would email that person and say, "Hey, I just read your article about your production company. I'm trying to learn about concert production. Could I buy you lunch when your tour comes through here? Ninety-nine out of one hundred people will never even reply.

If I didn't have the right DNA, I'd have given up long ago. But I continued to email the next guy, then the next one. Until one day somebody responded. People actually like to talk about what they do. So, he was excited to have me buy lunch. When I sat down with this guy and started talking to him about the concert industry, he offered to introduce me to his friend, Howard. Then after I meet with Howard, he says, "If you really want to learn about how to promote a concert, let me introduce you to my friend." So, you just need to get a foot in the door and start meeting people.

The point is, if you're not in their industry, most people assume there's no way to break in. Well, I say there's no way to break in if you don't even try.

So, I kept prodding, poking, pushing, cold emailing, and reading and eventually one little door opened. Once I was in, I started weaving my way through the network and meeting more people until one guy finally said, "I'm going to give you this huge Excel model that we use to actually plan and produce concerts."

It documented every little task you had to do! Suddenly, I had a workflow for producing a concert, which I'd never seen before.

I didn't do anything anybody can't do. I did something most other people won't do. I fought through a ton of rejection, and I worked like hell late at night, many nights.

When I started exploring getting into the music biz, people were once again telling me that I was nuts. "You're a tech guy. What are you doing? You know nothing about the music industry."

But imagine this: You go to a concert, and you think to yourself, "Man, how cool would it be to produce a concert someday?" So, the question becomes, can a software engineer without music experience produce a concert? Who knows? But not trying sits in your gut the rest of your life. So, we just went for it.

The first concert I produced all by myself was an Elton John concert that sold out in ten minutes. I went on stage and introduced him to twenty-eight thousand people. Apparently, the answer is yes. You can figure out how to produce a concert.

On a most basic level, we endeavor to engage with each other and with the world around us. In doing so, we connect to our humanity and what drives us. This was an unexpected story during my interview with Jeff not only because I didn't imagine hearing about promoting a concert after revolutionizing the travel industry, but because his literal way into the industry was by asking for advice.

Make It Real: Your "Ask for Advice" Challenge

Asking for advice isn't just about getting answers; it's about building relationships and creating opportunities that wouldn't exist otherwise.

Key Takeaways

- Asking for advice is a powerful way to build relationships and open doors.
- Honesty and vulnerability help establish trust. If you're nervous or intimidated, acknowledge it.
- Do your research before reaching out. People appreciate thoughtful, relevant questions.
- Curiosity leads to connections and opportunities.

Your Action Plan

- Make a list. Write down five people—whether in your industry or the new field you're curious about—whom you admire and would love to learn from.

- Do your research. Find out something specific about each person's work, background, or achievements that you can explore more deeply in a conversation.
- Draft your outreach. Write a short email or message to them asking for a coffee, where you can ask their advice on something relevant to their expertise.
  - Keep it simple, authentic, and specific (e.g., "If you were in my shoes, how would you approach X?").

AI Prompt: "I'm trying to get advice about [insert issue or decision]. Help me write a short, respectful message to someone more experienced—include my context, my top one to two questions, and why I'd value their perspective."

SEE THE FUTURE AS TRUE

Many thought leaders emphasize the power of visualization, arguing that deeply believing in a desired reality creates the conditions for it to manifest.

This principle can be applied to anything you want. For an entrepreneur, having a clear vision is a key skill in accessing High Five Energy. For me, it was clear that for RideAmigos and Vyng, there was zero chance of things not working out. In fact, in my reality, there is no way for it *not* to happen because it *already has*. No doubts. That is how I choose to live my life.

Believe Ain't Always Easy

Even with the ubiquitous acceptance of this concept, truly believing in something before it happens isn't always easy. Simply wanting to manifest a "dream job" or "a partner" or an "ideal home" are amorphic ideas that aren't easy to sink your teeth into.

I wondered if there was a way to make that concept more tangible. Visualization and meditation are in the mind... What if I could anchor a physical sensation to an experience rather than relying solely on an abstract thought?

OG High Five Energy

Before High Five Energy became the defining term to describe the founder flow state embodied in these pages, it was a personal hack of mine—a short-cut of sorts to help embody the vision of the future I desire.

To explore this concept in its simplest application, let's say I'm looking for a parking space. Instead of focusing solely on the *idea* of finding it, maybe I see my car parked on the curb.... What if I created the physical feeling of a sustained high-five with my friend when it happens? When I experience holding a high-five, I can feel the tingle in my hand, I can feel my heart race at the excitement of the win, and the real smile on my face lightens my spirit. That high-five is *very* real, it's now, it's this moment. I can ground myself in that feeling, anchoring my vision in something tangible.

When I was envisioning selling Vyng, Paul and I utilized OG High Five Energy. I could hold onto that feeling of Paul's hand hitting mine, and the energy running through my body as that slap sent a physical signal of success through me. I could create that high-five with another person or recall that sense memory when I'm alone. It's a shortcut to access manifestation energy and *see the future as true.*

Always There When You Need It

From parking spaces to acquisitions, OG High Five Energy is always at your fingertips...literally. It's a grounding practice and an easy hack for getting that visualization magic activated within you.

The Future You Want Is Inevitable—If You Believe It

No one embodies that mindset more than Minnie Ingersoll, an entrepreneur and venture capitalist best known for co-founding the Access team, which later evolved into Google Fiber, and for co-founding Shift, an online marketplace for used cars, where she served as chief operating officer. Minnie is now a partner at TenOneTen Ventures and above all else, loves silent disco and karaoke (the places where we bond the hardest). Once she sees the potential of what she can create, she relentlessly pushes forward, bringing her vision to life through sheer force of will, problem-solving, and an unshakable belief in what's possible.

> I had been working at Google, and had a nice stable job. In 2012/2013, when seed investment was less established, I had been writing some angel checks to my friends who were leaving Google to start companies. When I was seven months pregnant with my first child, I was going to sell my BMW as well as check on my investments. One of them was my friend, George, who was at the very beginning stages of starting Shift, called Shift Cars back then.

When I went to sell my car—and at that point, maybe I was eight or even nine months along, I was very pregnant—I posted on Craigslist. That's what you did back then. People would show up to your house, then you were expected to jump in the passenger seat, while they drive the car really fast. My husband was a consultant, so he was never home, and being so pregnant, the whole process felt unsafe. I even wondered if I should just give them the keys, but then realized they could drive off with my car.

So, I texted George, who would later become my co-founder at Shift, saying, "I totally see what you mean about the Craigslist experience being broken. How's my investment?" He was still fine-tuning the strategy, and I said, "But are you selling cars yet?" He wasn't.

Shortly after that conversation, I gave birth to my first child. My plan was to take seven months of maternity leave. About two months in, I was getting antsy. So, I started showing up at George's house and checking in on the business. I'm an operational person. He's an amazing strategic thinker. It wasn't long before I became the COO. I'd wake up at 5:00 AM, have five hours with the baby, and then I'd be at his house by 10:00 AM.

For me, having something new to sink my teeth into during my maternity leave was a huge gift. I just got intoxicated with startup life. I'd been at Google for a third of my life at that point—I was thirty-six, I'd been there twelve years. I was a product manager most of my career. The stars aligned, and I was well suited to create what was needed to get us up and running.

At the time, everyone's picking off pieces of Craigslist, expanding upon different verticals. For example, instead of finding a babysitter on Craigslist, you go to Care.com. We were the "selling your car" piece of that. Buying and, more specifically, selling your used car was very difficult to do on Craigslist. Most people didn't know how to price their cars. Similarly, people didn't know how much to spend when buying a car. There wasn't good data. Both buyer and seller felt they got the short end of the stick at the end of the experience.

There must be a better way of doing this. Especially because used car sales is a trillion-dollar industry. It's huge. Yet only 1 percent of car sales were done online.

Our starting point was to offer help by attaching financing and securing warranties for people selling their cars online. Something dealerships could offer in person, but not Craigslist. The initial business consisted of people selling their cars for more than $10,000, so financing and some sort of warranty was highly desired.

Our original premise was: we will come to your house, do a quick inspection, which would allow you to sell it with financing and a warranty. We started with around ten customers a month for a few months, and what happened very quickly was that more than half of them were asking if we could just take the cars off their hands. They didn't want to deal with it. "Thanks for the financing, the warranty, and the inspection. Really, I just don't want to sell this car myself." Because our friend group were our first customers, there was a level of trust and buy-in allowing us to pivot and start taking the cars, without giving them money. But when I look back, it's a bit surprising that we were able to pull it off.

This was a true start-up in every sense of the word. At the time, my sixteen-year-old nephew, who looked fourteen, worked for us going to pick up the cars from customers' homes. We gave out business cards that looked so janky along with a printed piece of paper that said, "We promise to pay you when your car sells." My nephew looked like he could barely drive, and there he was, picking up Porsches, in exchange for a promise to pay later. It was one of the big tests: Would people give their car without getting money? You could look up my LinkedIn and see that I worked at Google, but the desire to offload the cars was greater than the questions of our legitimacy.

Soon, we had a ton of cars parked outside George's apartment. Which was a pain in the ass, and the reason for raising our Series A; we had to get a real warehouse. We couldn't keep track of the cars! There were many moments of "Is this our Corolla?" while aiming the key fob at different ones parked on the street. We first moved from outside of George's house to Costco, which in San Francisco allowed you to rent monthly. But in order to get a real warehouse and to expand beyond thirty cars in inventory, we needed real financing.

Sometimes you have the two-sided marketplace problem where you have to get both sides going. Interestingly for us, we didn't have that problem because we could always sell the cars we acquired on Craigslist. While ShiftCars.com was in operation, no one ever went there to look for cars. We had no SEO compared to Craigslist or many other places. What's remarkable is if we were selling twenty-five cars a month, we were at almost $3 million in revenue, or GMV, gross merchandise value. From a top-line revenue perspective, just with hustling twenty-five cars a month, we started to look like a real company.

Being in the Bay area, we were finding that a lot of people buying Teslas needed a way to get rid of their existing car because Tesla won't take trade-ins of any car other than another Tesla. We recognized the opportunity and staffed the six or seven Tesla dealerships in the Bay Area with two of my nephews and a bunch of college interns. Every morning we'd have them show up with donuts or bagels and make friends with the general manager. We were positioning ourselves to be the go-to person for trading-in used gas-powered cars. Offer a seamless, white-glove service to make the process effortless for sellers. That was our vision.

George has a remarkable ability to decide something is possible or necessary and then manifest it. And I see this all the time where human potential is concerned. I see time and time again people saying, "I know this is what I need. I know this is what the world needs. I know this is what I want." And then they do it. The Tesla partnership is what we wanted. From four people in George's apartment taking notes on a whiteboard seeing so clearly: they needed us and we needed them. We finally found someone who knew someone who knew someone who knew the head of Tesla sales. Until we came along, Tesla didn't have a good experience for people selling their used cars. We were a good fit; we did a ton of prep and secured a partnership. Because of that partnership with Tesla, we secured our Series A. We networked our way into the global head of sales at Tesla just by hustling.

I see it in pitches all the time now, when great entrepreneurs have a vision and can articulate it clearly, then they can get there.

At our peak, we reached a $1 billion valuation. We went public through a SPAC, brought in a new CEO, and as this transition was underway, I realized what I could offer the company had reached its max. In retrospect, I was lucky that I had already exited because we struggled as a public company. Meanwhile, our closest competitor and crosstown rival, Carvana, thrived. What's interesting is that our business models were quite similar, yet we never reached profitability or hit that escape velocity. Carvana, on the other hand, managed to break through, especially in terms of brand awareness now worth around $50 billion.

My time at Google, along with my experience in the startup world—both as a founder and now an investor— has shaped a fundamental question for me: Why bother to build a business if you're not actually optimizing for the goodness of people's lives? When the success of Shift came at the expense of our workforce, needing to go from W-2s to 1099s, essentially transitioning to cheap labor, it made me question if I even want to build a business that can't provide great health care to every employee.

Sometimes we get so caught up in the idea that the startup is the baby, but at the end of the day, it's about whether or not that business is creating value holistically.

It's easier for me as an investor to see that. What's the whole point of building a business if it's not to enhance people's lives? Starting with the people who work there. Work is such a big part of life. At least let's make sure that work is a really positive force in someone's life.

At its core, Minnie's story is about envisioning a new way of doing something and seeing it through to fruition. She and George started with a clear belief in the potential of transforming the used car sales market. When it came to the vision of a future partnership with Tesla, a pretty ambitious goal, each step they took toward making it happen was fueled by the understanding that it was possible. Because anything is possible. The partnership, much like the startup's evolution, was sustained by the clarity of what the team wanted and the relentless drive to make it real. Seeing the future as true helps to imbue you with the agility required to push, pivot, adapt and create what you desire.

Make It Real: Your "See the Future as True" Challenge

Key Takeaways

- Visualization is a powerful tool, but belief makes it real.
- Attach a physical sensation, like a high five, to anchor a vision into your body, making it more tangible.

Your Action Plan:

1. Pick a goal. Choose something you want to manifest (hooking that investor, hiring the best COO, or having a successful launch).

2. Create the feeling. Visualize it already happening. Let yourself see it. Hear it. Feel it. Picture the room, the sounds, the celebration, the calm confidence. Let the success live in your body for a moment—as if it's already real.

3. Anchor it physically. Find someone you trust—a cofounder, a friend, a teammate—and give them a high five, but don't let go. Hold it. Stay in contact for a few seconds. Feel the warmth between your palms. Feel the shared intention in that moment. Let the energy of what you're creating flow between you—from your hand, through your body, into the world.

AI Prompt: "Act like I've already achieved my biggest vision. Describe my life, work, and impact three years from now—based on my current goals in [insert area]. Make it vivid, detailed, and written in the present tense."

Want to watch the full interview with Minnie Ingersoll?
Visit: www.jeffreychernick.com

LEARNING IS IN THE DOING

"I had ten times the learning experience running my own
startup than I did at a large tech company. The intensity—
the 'brain on fire' feeling—was unmatched. I had gone
to business school, but nothing prepares you for being
the COO like getting your hands dirty and doing it."

—Minnie Ingersoll, co-founder of Shift.com ($415 million SPAC)

Excluding niche industries like space, starting a business most
likely won't cost you very much. A simple landing page, a social
media campaign, or even a pre-sale model can help validate
demand before spending a ton of time and resources on development. When entrepreneurs come to me with extensive plans
and huge budgets, before knowing if they even have product
market fit, I remind them that you can test most business ideas
for free. Many successful companies started with basic proto-
types, self-funded experiments, or even just a concept tested

through direct customer conversations. With today's digital tools, it's easier than ever to test most ideas.

Not All Ideas Are Good Ideas

That's how you find out that not all ideas are great ideas. While I've had good ideas like the taxi sharing website and the video ringtone app, I've had *other* ideas too.

On a sunny California day, while lying on the beach, the wind kept lifting up and folding my towel over itself. Sand was blowing all over it and on me… At that moment I thought, "Wouldn't it be cool if the towel held its shape once I laid it down?" The idea for Mali-Towel was born. Mali-Towel—a.k.a. "malleable towel"—would be a beach towel that holds the form you create for it.

In its early ideation phase, I thought Mali-Towel was a great idea that had several use cases for pools and beaches. After partnering with a good friend who was interested in learning more about entrepreneurship, I met someone who owned an invention company. For $500 each, we commissioned a prototype.

Create an MVP

We created what's called an MVP, a minimum viable product. That means creating the simplest form of your idea to interact with, and potentially even have a customer experience it. From there, you can get a sense of whether or not it is something worth pursuing.

After exploring around ten iterations, the final product was a towel with a malleable wire sewn along the edges enabling the user to create and hold the towel's form. I was *so* excited when the first Mali-Towel arrived at my door. I opened the package, held it up in the sunlight… and realized Mali-Towel was an "okay" idea. There was *no way* in hell I was going to work on that concept for the next two to five years of my life.

Test, and Move On

What's valuable here is that I took the initial steps required to test my idea. Rather than let the next best thing since sliced bread sit in the back of my mind for years, I took action to test my hypothesis. It doesn't make sense to invest exorbitant amounts of time, capital, and resources into an untested idea, but you can take smaller, initial steps that help to reveal if you are on the right track.

Passion Matters

This story ties back into another important theme: With any entrepreneurial idea, it is helpful to pursue something you are passionate about. This is because that idea could be something you're going to work on for years to come. Success typically requires that this new idea become the center of your life. And because nothing happens as quickly as you think it's going to, having a clear vision and *passion* for what you are creating is key in maintaining the drive to see it through.

In the case of Mali-Towel…it was not worth pursuing.

However, the Mali-Towel experiment was *not* a waste of time. The process of discovering that it *wasn't* for me was valuable in and of itself. From real world data and experience, I was able to definitively decide not to move forward. Data is data. Failures in business and entrepreneurship provide tangible lessons that you can apply to future endeavours, and they ultimately serve to create the foundation for future success. So, I passed on that one and moved on to my next.

Another quick story from my interview with Brian Lee—this one is about the founding of ShoeDazzle.

Sometimes it's better not to know too much and to be somewhat of an outsider. You approach things differently than people who are insiders, or who know the industry well. The perfect example of that is ShoeDazzle.

I thought doing a "shoe of the month club" was a great idea because I saw how much money my wife spent on shoes. And how addicted she was to shoes. So, I started thinking, "If we make affordable shoes available through a monthly subscription, it could work." We raised capital on the idea, and we had Kim Kardashian ready to start promoting. We had the website built; we had everything ready except for the inventory. We had no shoes!

Someone told me that all you have to do is go to the City of Industry, and you'll see all these warehouses and you can get whatever shoes you need. They manufacture in China or Asia but have showrooms where you can buy the shoes. So, I'm thinking, that's the easy part.

I remember we drove out to the City of Industry. We go in and we're exploring the merchandise, looking at all these shoes, thinking, *Oh, this is fantastic.*

After looking around, we connected with a sales rep and said, "We'll take fifty pairs of this. We'll take a hundred pairs of that. We'll take twenty pairs of this one. Oh, and can you put the ShoeDazzle logo on them?" And they look at us like we're nuts.

They say, "Where are you from?" We reply, "We're from ShoeDazzle." With raised brows they look at me and say, "No, the minimum order is five thousand pairs. Per style, per color."

I'm stunned. We had to stop everything. We had to go find a partner who would make small batch runs for us. Something we thought would be easy. But we finally found that partner, which ended up delaying us by about six months.

I remember after we launched, we went to our first shoe convention called World Shoe Association, WSA in Las Vegas—it was a huge convention.

It took up two convention centers: the Las Vegas Convention Center and the Mandalay Bay. The sheer size of it was so daunting that I'm pretty convinced if I had seen it before starting ShoeDazzle, I would have never started ShoeDazzle. I've never seen *so* many people in my life selling shoes. That scared the bejesus out of me. It was a rude awakening. I realized I'm competing against a lot of people selling shoes. But it was too late to turn back at that point.

> Then we started building, and it took off like a rocket when we launched.
>
> Kim Kardashian was instrumental in its success. She was a great business partner. She's one of the hardest working women I know. She has an incredible fan base because she's just a likable person, but she's also really professional. She shows up.

The very nature of the venture—starting without knowing all the details and learning on the go—illustrates how hands-on experience is a great teacher. Brian didn't come from the shoe industry, so he approached it with fresh eyes and perhaps a bit of naivete. His initial mistake of assuming it would be easy to acquire shoes and launch the business shows that entrepreneurship involves a lot of trial and error. It's through doing, failing, and adapting that he learned the ropes.

Make It Real: "Learning Is in the Doing" Challenge

Diving in, making mistakes, pivoting, and pushing forward are part of the entrepreneurship game.

Key Takeaways

- Learning happens through action. Experience is the best teacher.
- Testing ideas with small, low-cost experiments helps validate them before committing significant resources.
- Not all ideas are good ideas, and that's okay. Each experiment builds knowledge and clarity.

- Passion is key. If you're not excited to dedicate years to an idea, it's probably not the right one.

Your Action Plan

1. Define an MVP. What's the simplest, cheapest way to test if there's demand? A landing page, a social media post, a quick prototype?
2. Test it. Take one small action in the next twenty-four hours to test your idea in the real world.
3. Reflect. What did you learn? Did it spark excitement, or do you feel relieved to move on?
4. Iterate or drop. If the response is promising, what's the next experiment? If not, what's your next idea?

AI Prompt: "I've been stuck researching [insert topic/skill/idea]. Help me turn this into a thirty-day action plan where I learn by doing—with weekly goals and simple steps I can actually follow."

THE MIND GROUP

"I try to hire or find co-founders that are creative thinkers. Build a leadership team that will tell me what I don't want to hear."

—Stephen Kaufer, co-founder of TripAdvisor
($2 billion market cap)

Let's say you are dropped in the Amazon and told to make it to the other side of the jungle. Machete in hand, how do you proceed?

The Hard Way or the Easy(er) Way

The way I see it, there are two main categories you can fall into:

- The Independent Path: Some people have something to prove. "I want to be my own person. I don't need anyone else to be successful. I'll hack my way through that jungle and reach the other side. I may run into poisonous snakes, but I'll make it—earning the respect I deserve!"

- The Supported Path: Then there's the person who, before stepping foot into the jungle, seeks out a local village in search of experts. Hunters and guides who can offer advice. Maybe they can even persuade a guide to show them the way. There is a good chance that someone has already made the trek. Why not benefit from their experience?

What Is the Mind Group?

Therein lies the lesson. Whether I'm starting a company or pursuing a goal, someone has likely faced similar challenges. So, why not build a network of experts in the field I'm navigating? Even if I ultimately choose a different path, I'll be armed with valuable insights from those who have already been there.

I call this group of advisors the Mind Group. With the benefit of collective knowledge culled from various sources, pursuing your goals is easier, more efficient, and less stressful than trying to hack through life with a machete on your own.

A Real-World Example: JFK

A famous example of this concept is when President John F. Kennedy surrounded himself with a team of advisors often described as "the best and the brightest." He intentionally sought out individuals who were not only highly intelligent but who also brought diverse perspectives and expertise, ensuring that his administration avoided the pitfalls of an echo chamber.

This approach was particularly successful during critical moments like the Cuban Missile Crisis, where his inner circle—known as ExComm—had rigorous debates, offering competing viewpoints and played a crucial role in advising Kennedy on how to handle the Soviet Union's placement of nuclear missiles in Cuba, which brought the world to the brink of nuclear war. Kennedy's willingness to be challenged and to foster an environment where differing opinions were valued serves as a map for building a circle of people who push you to think bigger.

The Power of Collective Advice

When new challenges arise, I call on those advisors who I have built relationships with using the tools in this book. I take their collective advice and, combined with my own reasoning and experience, make the most informed decisions at my disposal, thus, allowing me to circumvent unnecessary challenges and make it to the other side.

When it comes to your entrepreneurial pursuits, your *professional* Mind Group will typically be your co-founders, colleagues, and mentors sourced from your professional network. However, there is a well-known idea: "You are the average of the five people you hang out with most."

Let's Get Personal

Perhaps more of an unconscious influence on your life, your *personal* Mind Group is composed of, whether you intended it or not, your best friends. The people you spend time with most shape your thinking, can challenge your ideas, and either propel you forward or hold you back. If, for example, the people you hang out with are uninspired, lazy, and lack ambition, it may be hard for you to break that mold (though nothing is impossible). If the people around you are driven, crushing it career-wise, and innovative, then it is very likely they will inspire you to level up your game and continue to strive for new heights.

In any case, choose the people around you with intention. Leverage the knowledge base of those that came before you, and put down the machete every now and then for that shortcut on your left.

In my interview with Jack Dangermond, he reveals a network of support that enabled him to create Esri and become the co-founder and entrepreneur he is today. Jack's success is a testament to how powerful the Mind Group approach can be.

It started with my folks. They were immigrants from Holland with a sixth-grade education. My mother was a maid; my father was a gardener. While working very hard as servants, here in our little town, Redlands, one of the people that they worked for said, "Pete and Alice, you should send your kids to college."

My parents didn't know what that even meant. But they figured that they would start a little nursery business in order to make enough money to send us to college. They started first by taking cuttings and propagating them in their backyard of their little old house on the north side of Redlands. At the end of the war, they sold that house and bought a piece of land out on West Redlands in the orange groves, along with an old army surplus tent.

With used plywood from the Salvation Army, they built a little office building and lived there, while the kids lived in the tent.

They started selling plants. It was really a bold thing to do. We lived there for my entire life until I went to college. They taught me everything. They taught me how to sell. They taught me how to grow things, how to nurture things, making sure that plants were always watered, weeded…how things should be taken care of in the nursery. We didn't have much in the beginning, but as customers would buy plants, they would reinvest all of their sales into buying new plants, learning how to grow, buy, and sell plants and later sell landscape services.

They built that from basically nothing, no money, just lots of hard work, day and night. They kept their servants' jobs, as well, so growing up in a family like that, watching them work like crazy and create value from nothing, was an amazing education. I learned everything that I know about business in that nursery. Taking out deliveries, working with customers to design their backyards, selling them plants, knowing how to help them realize a beautiful landscape around their homes. Learning how to upsell, or cross-sell as we call it today. But in those days, of course, it was just "making a living." It put all of us kids through college.

Once I got into college, I just barely made it in, but once I got into college, I learned computing in undergraduate. I learned geography at Minnesota. I learned computer mapping at Harvard and the whole concepts of GIS. Notably, I learned how to learn from different professors who had taken an interest. When somebody does that, it's very motivating. Carl Steinitz, who pioneered geodesign, and Howard Fisher, who invented the first computer mapping software, took an interest in me, nurtured me, and helped me; that was very valuable. I stand on their shoulders.

With my career, the same thing happened. I had an appetite for learning, so every business engagement I had, I learned something. When I started Esri, feedback from our customers was an invaluable resource as well as advice from my peers. I learned painfully about cash flow by having a customer—the government of Puerto Rico—that didn't pay me for seven months. And it almost crushed me at the beginning.

An engineer I worked with, about three years in, that had his own ten or fifteen person engineering company, said to me, "Jack, when you're in business for yourself, you only have to know three things."

One-third of your time has to be spent on sales and marketing, making sure you know how to sell your vision, your work, your product. The second third of your time has to be spent on building the products and making sure they're good quality, and that you deliver on time, and you keep your agreements. The final third of your time has to be spent on cash flow, making sure you have revenue to pay your wages. He said, "Selling, doing, and collecting the money." Those were the three big lessons. And sure enough, whether you're ten people, which we were at that time, or whether you're ten thousand people, which we have now, as an owner, you need to spend one-third of your time on each of those efforts. It's very unique to find a person that can actually do all three.

In fact, it is so unique that it almost never happens. For whatever reason, growing up in the nursery, I learned how to sell; I learned how to deliver, grow things, and nurture things; and learned how to balance that ambition with money that actually can support it.

That balance is the key to creating and running a self-perpetuating company, a self-sustaining company. Again, almost impossible. Few people get lucky to do it, but having the intention from the beginning is very important.

Jack's support started with his parents, whose relentless work ethic and entrepreneurial spirit instilled in him foundational business principles he carried into his career. They weren't traditional mentors in the academic sense, but their hands-on teaching in their nursery business nurtured his skills in sales, allowing him to grow and reinvest back into the business. His support continued through the guidance of mentors, clients, and peers whose influence helped shape his trajectory. His story showcases the importance of learning from those who came before you, seeking intentional mentorship, and surrounding yourself with individuals who challenge and inspire you to grow.

Make It Real: Your "Mind Group" Challenge

The Mind Group is about creating a network of smart people you can actively learn from.

Key Takeaways

- Surround yourself with experts. Leverage the wisdom and experience of others who have already navigated similar terrain.
- Diversify. Leaning on a diverse group of advisors, mentors, and peers can help you make better, more informed decisions.
  - Build a support system that challenges you and offers you a different way to look at something.
- Your BFFs shape your experience. Beyond your professional network, the people you spend the most time with socially have a profound impact on your thinking and your ability to achieve your goals.
- Intentionality is key. Whether in your professional or personal life, be intentional about who you spend time with.

Your Action Plan: Audit and Build Your Mind Group

1. Map your current Mind Group. List out the people you turn to for advice, both personally and professionally.
2. Audit your network. Review the people you spend the most time with. Are they helping you grow or holding you back? Are they diverse in thought and expertise?

3. Identify gaps. Based on your audit, are there any gaps in your Mind Group? Perhaps you need someone who excels in a different area.

4. Set intentional goals. Identify two to three people you want to add to your Mind Group or strengthen your relationships with.

5. Take action. Reach out to someone who can help you fill a gap or provide support in a key area. Whether through mentorship, collaboration, or simply a deeper conversation, take the first step toward strengthening your Mind Group.

AI Prompt: "Help me identify the five kinds of people I should have in my personal and professional Mind Group—based on my current goals in [insert area]. Include traits, experience, and what each one could help me see or avoid."

You technically *can* succeed in isolation. But it's much harder, and this *is* a book about behavioral shifts that get you where you want to go, faster.

WRITE YOUR OWN NARRATIVE

I learned my first hack on the sales desk.

Let's say I had a prospective client in Miami, Florida. There's only so much I can do over the phone. To close a deal, it's best to meet in person. The challenge is how to get that first face-to-face meeting. You shouldn't spend time and money flying from city to city, hoping for a close—it must be strategic.

The Anchor Meeting Strategy

My boss from Lehman Brothers, Sandy, taught me a simple but powerful trick—create a reason to be there. Instead of asking a prospect outright for a meeting, I'd say, "Hey, I'm actually going to be in Florida the second or third week of February. Do you have fifteen minutes to grab coffee?" The stakes are low, and there's no pressure on the prospect. You are in town anyway, so why not?

Once I confirmed the first commitment—what I called the Anchor Meeting—I built an entire trip around it. That first big meeting (the whale) made the trip legitimate, and from there, I could book more meetings with other prospects, continuing to build my network, and potentially close a deal. One commitment turned into a fully justified business trip. Saying that I will already be in Florida is a sly but harmless way to ease the pressure off an executive I'm attempting to meet.

Creating Opportunities Instead of Waiting for Them

I didn't have a reason to be in Florida until I created one. This strategy, of course, is not limited to prospects. Use it to create meetings when building out your network. If you need to be in Florida, don't wait for Florida to come to you—there's of course no guarantee that it ever will.

Serving Deals on Ice

I met the founder of a Korean pear juice startup, Seoul Juice, while guest speaking at a Pepperdine MBA class on entrepreneurship. He approached me after the session, and I eventually came on board as an advisor. A year later, I stepped in to help lead the seed raise. We got invited to a high-end investor event, and I told the founder, Luis, to bring plenty of product. Then I went to Kinko's and printed our deal terms on cardboard menus—the kind usually used for cocktail bars. It was bold, and no one had ever seen that move before. Investors loved it. The product made a strong impression—and paired with that kind of ingenuity and hustle, we closed the round sixty days later.

Publish Without Permission

This is your invitation to get creative and do things your own way.

Not unlike how Lynda Weinman, in the early days leading up to Lynda.com, didn't take no for an answer and achieved her vision in unexpected and creative ways.

I got very interested in how to explain to people how to make a website. How to create the graphics and how to add video… I enjoyed educating people on all that went into creating a website with impact. That was what my first book was about. When I initially made a proposal to a publisher, they rejected it. I could not get a single book publisher interested. Knowing that the information was valuable and that people would want to learn how to create a website, I had to figure out how to get the information out another way. So, I made a proposal to a magazine. Rather than one large book, I suggested publishing it in installations. I secured a deal with a magazine to let me do each chapter as an installment. And that's how I got a magazine to publish my web design articles.

Then a year later, I had a bidding war over the same book proposal, which was already written thanks to my publishing deal with the magazine and for which I'd gotten paid to write. I was always figuring out how to get paid to do the things I loved. I couldn't just do things for free because I needed to pay my rent. I was just really crafty; I had to figure out ways to take no prisoners. No matter what, I was going to get this idea out there.

Lynda's ability to craft her own narrative and create opportunities when traditional doors were slammed in her face reflects the epitome of the entrepreneurial spirit. She didn't wait for validation from publishers; instead, she found an alternative route to bringing her ambition to life while staying true to her authentic vision. You'll start to notice with entrepreneurs that how we do one thing is how we do everything. That same "craftiness" Lynda used to publish her book via installments in a magazine is another entrepreneurial archetype that appears again and again throughout her journey.

Make It Real: Your "Write Your Own Narrative" Challenge

Key Takeaways

- Opportunities don't always appear on their own, you have to create them.
- Taking control of your narrative allows you to align your actions with your goals and turn obstacles into opportunities.
- Waiting for permission is a losing game. Find alternate routes (or make them).

Your Action Plan:

- How is your effort to build your Mind Group going? Need a boost?
- Apply the Anchor Meeting Strategy and book some meetings.
- Who can you reach out to, what can you propose, or how can you shift your approach to make it happen?

AI Prompt: "I have an idea I believe in, but traditional paths (like venture funding, tech resources, or marketing) are not available. Help me brainstorm three creative, scrappy ways to get this idea out into the world anyway—while staying true to my vision."

UNDERSTAND YOUR TARGET MARKET

Within your list of ideas you've since created, you may have a few top contenders to choose from. Now, even if they are cool, innovative, or useful concepts, it's important to suss out if there's a viable market. The question is: Are people going to want what you are selling? And if the desire is there, is it strong enough to warrant spending resources to create it? To answer these questions, it is important to speak with potential customers. For Jampling, while I was in the ideation phase, I called HR reps to vet the idea. For the Mali-Towel, I asked my community if they'd use such a product.

A Mentee's Example

A great example isn't directly mine: I was paired with my mentee in NFTE, a summer program in Los Angeles that pairs entrepreneurs with middle and high school students in low-income areas to mentor them in entrepreneurship. Kenneth had an idea for a waterless car wash mobile app. He was in high school at the time, envisioning an app that would allow people, from the comfort of their homes, to order a carwash, with no water. With the use of special wipes that he had sourced from a supplier, his business model was to license the app to car wash facilities. There, they could have their own white-labeled app and could be able to expand their services locally.

An Idea Is Great Until You Test It

Cool idea? For sure, it definitely had potential. On our first day together, I asked if he had ever spoken to a carwash owner about the concept. He said no. Kenneth could have spent the next "X" amount of time blindly developing this business plan without input from the very people who would become his customers. We hopped in my car and drove to the nearest car wash where we asked to speak with the owner. The owner was there and had been in the car wash business for twenty years, working his way up from employee to owner. The man had car washing in his blood. And he knew the market well.

Kenneth pitched his idea, and in turn, received honest feedback on why it could work and why it wouldn't work—mostly the latter. Profit margins are super low for car washes. It's composed of old school ways of doing things. Getting these businesses on mobile apps would be a great challenge. The waterless car wash mobile app would be a completely new business model for these owners.

Kenneth and I said thank you, hopped back in the car, and drove to the school. This was not defeat; it was an insight.

Build Off What You Learn

We brainstormed and explored how we could pivot. What if the app provided an Uber-like experience for individual washers that joined the platform as contractors and if it serviced specific geographic areas? A user could order a waterless car wash on the app, a registered car washer in the area would be assigned to the job (using the registered supplies of the company), and the revenue would be split between parties. Just like Uber.

We ran the numbers, and the math made sense. After building his pitch, practicing, and tweaking further over the next two months, Kenneth went to the NFTE National Competition and came in second place, winning a cash prize, as well as a trip to DC where he met President Obama. I mean, what a dream! For both of us, really—I was super proud.

Kenneth did not end up pursuing the app further because he thought of an even bigger idea. A true entrepreneur—which I honor and applaud.

The Power of Feedback

If we hadn't made the important decision to meet a potential customer, who knows how Kenneth's journey would have unfolded. The lesson: get a sense of the market, meet your customers, and evolve your idea to accommodate the new information gained through that process.

In my interview with Brian Lee, he shared a story about his pivot to ProxiLaw that highlights the importance of truly understanding your target market. Knowing the desires of your target market isn't just valuable, it's *essential* for making informed decisions about which paths to take.

Around year two, we were doing well, we were growing a little bit here and there, and we were becoming profitable because we had to be. We really weren't taking big salaries, eating peanut butter and jelly sandwiches type of days.

We got kind of lucky because we fell into pay-per-click advertising on search engines very early. We were one of the earliest companies to do that, which helped us grow.

But soon we noticed that a customer from Florida ordered their twelfth divorce from us within four months. I remember being concerned, so I called him myself and said, "Hi, this is Brian from LegalZoom. I noticed that you have been divorced twelve times in three months, and I'm just checking up on you. How are things going?"

Admittedly, I was also curious about the type of person who gets divorced twelve times. He said, "I'm actually a family lawyer based in Florida, and I use LegalZoom for back end legal documents." Something akin to a digital paralegal. Of course, me and my business partner thought, "ding, ding, ding!" We're not just B2C to our consumers! We can build a more robust LegalZoom and sell software to attorneys so they can create very simple legal documents for their own clients!

Again, at this point, LegalZoom was doing fine, growing a little bit month over month, and we were profitable. In response to this new information, we decided to start a separate company that services attorneys, called ProxiLaw. We ended up taking our best resources, our best graphic designers, software engineers, best packaging, best everyone...and we put them into building the software for ProxiLaw. We saw it as the future. We were convinced we were going to make so much more money selling to lawyers, in part because we could charge more.

Sure enough, a year into it, we noticed LegalZoom kind of plateauing and dipping downwards actually, but we felt it was okay because we've got ProxiLaw.

After launching ProxiLaw, after about three or four months, we got eighteen attorneys to sign up. That was a terribly rough time because we thought we'd have at least five hundred attorneys signed up by that point. It was a rude awakening: what we failed to realize early on when we built it was that selling to lawyers is just very, very different than selling to consumers.

Customer acquisition was much more labor-intensive. We'd have to actually knock on attorneys' doors, show and explain the software, then try to convince them to move away from what they were doing to use this technology. Attorneys, especially at the time, were notoriously slow to embracing new technology. It was a tough go, and we were losing money hand over fist.

We went from profitable to very unprofitable. Because of ProxiLaw, we almost went under. We were very close to not making it. We had to stop taking salaries for a little while. We convinced some of our executives to stop taking salaries, but to stick with us. We eventually shut down ProxiLaw to refocus and reinvigorate our efforts on the mothership: LegalZoom.

And so, the lesson I've always carried with me is this: If you're working on something that's already working, keep your focus there. Double down, refine, and strengthen it until it's rock-solid. Only then should you think about branching out. Stay focused, go deeper, and build a solid foundation before you extend.

While Brian and his team had a strong grasp of their consumer base (B2C) with LegalZoom, they underestimated the significant differences when they shifted to a B2B model aimed at attorneys. They learned the hard way that every market has unique needs, buying behaviors, and barriers to adoption. Brian's story emphasizes the importance of thoroughly researching and validating your target market before throwing your all behind an endeavor. But in the end, it reinforces the value in entrepreneurial agility. By shutting down ProxiLaw and doubling down on their original vision, they were able to re-align with their target market and save LegalZoom.

Make It Real: "Understand Your Target Market" Challenge

Key Takeaways

- Understanding your target market is critical to ensuring the viability of your idea.
- Feedback is key. By getting feedback directly from potential customers, you can avoid wasting time and resources on concepts that may not be well-received.

Your Action Plan: Understand Your Target Market

Step 1: Identify Your Market

- Who are the potential users of your product or service?
- What are their primary needs and pain points?
- Where do they spend their time (online or offline)?

Step 2: Connect with Your Market

- Reach out to potential customers (via surveys, interviews, social media groups, or in-person meetings).
- Ask open-ended questions to uncover their true needs, motivations, and opinions.
- Listen more than you talk. What are they saying, and what they *aren't* saying (e.g., concerns or doubts they might not voice directly)?

Step 3: Analyze the Feedback

- What recurring themes or patterns did you notice in the feedback you received?

- What was the most surprising insight you learned from your conversations?
- Is there any way to tweak your product or service to better meet the needs of your target market?

AI Prompt: "I'm building a product/service for [describe your audience]. Help me create a detailed customer persona—including their daily struggles, decision-making habits, what motivates them to take action, and what kind of questions I should ask during interviews. Now act like one of these customers. I'll pitch you what I'm working on—tell me what resonates, what feels off, and what would actually make you want to buy."

THINK OUTSIDE THE BOX

I once decided to raise $8,000 to build a clean water well in Peru.

The Initial Strategy

- First, I emailed every single person I knew.
- I posted videos on social media.
- I even threw a few parties to raise awareness and funds for my cause.

At the $6,000 mark, I had exhausted my contacts. Many had donated ten to twenty dollars with a few larger contributions interspersed among them.

Time to Think Differently

To be honest, I found myself frustrated with my ceiling and knew I needed to think outside of the box; I needed to expand my scope of possibility beyond my usual way of doing things. One day, after work at Vyng, I turned to my co-founder, Sohrab, who by trade is a filmmaker, and proclaimed that I was not going to drink water for twenty-four hours. (I had heard the max-limit before your health is put in jeopardy is seventy-two hours, so I figured it would be a piece of cake.) The challenge began, I started posting about it on Facebook.

The donations came trickling in. However, it wasn't moving fast enough. I needed to up the ante, create a *pop* to get people's attention.

Keep Pushing New Ideas

On a whim, Sohrab and I thought of a ploy to grab people's attention and close the gap. Turning on Facebook Live, I handed my phone to Sohrab, and we headed off to the supermarket. I walked around, engaging with strangers, telling them what I was fighting for. "Did you know that 785 million people—one in nine—lack access to safe water? And 1.8 billion people currently use a source of drinking water contaminated by feces."

Yeah, most people don't know that. I also explained how I hadn't been drinking water for almost twenty hours to raise awareness for the cause (and I was *super* thirsty). As more people started viewing my Facebook Live, I upped the ante again by drinking dirty water à la dirt from the parking lot (gross, I know), eating hot nacho Cheez-Its, and even accepting a viewer's challenge of eating a bunch of cinnamon, a.k.a. the Cinnamon Challenge.

It Paid Off (Thankfully!)

By the end of the evening, I had educated random shoppers on a Wednesday night at my local supermarket and raised the remaining $2,000 needed to fund the well. Generosity.org, the nonprofit organization behind the cause, awarded me the "Innovation Award" at their annual gala a few months later.

If it's not clear by now, I'll say it again: thinking outside the box and leveraging all the tools you have at your disposal is an essential mindset that will get you far in the pursuit of what you're after. As in this case, my ceiling turned out to be an invitation to expand beyond what I thought was possible and get creative, even when it seemed that I had exhausted all my options.

My interview with Darren Berkovitz, co-founder of Telesign ($330 million exit), the company that introduced two-factor authentication for digital identity verification, revealed an "outside the box" strategy that is largely responsible for turning the tide in his venture from a good idea to a successful company.

Put yourself in the 2005 mindset, BI: before iPhone. Security is going to be a big problem on the internet. Today that seems obvious, we hear about breaches all day. But, at the time it wasn't. No one was talking about security. We figured that having everything stored in your email was incredibly risky. So, we set out to answer

---

the question, "How can we protect people in a way that removes the internet from the equation?"

Out of college, I found an accelerator in LA to hire me. While living at home and getting paid very little, we began to incubate ideas. The original idea for Telesign was: you place an automated voice call, (this was before SMS) saying a code, the person would then enter it in, and that's it, and you are verified. Today, everyone takes that for granted, noting how you've probably been verified three times this morning. Back then, there were a few people doing somewhat similar things, but we were in uncharted waters. We paid a company in Israel to do the voice calls, paying them twenty-five cents a voice call, and we tried to sell them for eight cents a voice call. Only losing seventeen cents a transaction, we continued to iterate from there. Eventually we offered SMS, continuing to navigate the naysayers. We heard over and over that no one will be using SMS.

We knew we had a good idea, but there was no external validation. People were saying, "No, we don't need this." Some were quite mean saying, "Go get a real job. This is horrible. This is never going to work." Despite the noise, in the back of my mind, I always knew security was going to be an issue. This is just human nature.

We were ahead of the market, but having humorous co-founders can help a lot of that roll off your back. Celebrating the smallest of wins—like a guy just calling me back—kept us going. It took three grueling years to turn Telesign into a real business, but in 2008, we finally got our big break.

The first company to integrate our technology was one of the most trafficked websites in the world. We had no money and had to hack our way into partnerships by sending cold emails. It's free. At first, we started gathering emails ourselves. Then, we found teams in India and Eastern Europe that would work all night, gathering emails, ready for our use in the morning.

I finally cold emailed the CTO of that website, and he hit me right back. Whoa. It turns out, they were having a big problem with people posting spam. Every time you go on their site and click a spam message, spammers make money, upwards of hundreds of thousands of dollars. The CTO explained that nothing they had tried worked. We posed: What if we make you verify your phone number before you post? That would limit one phone number per post. If you're a legitimate person, that's fine. If you're not, now you would need one hundred phone numbers to do one hundred posts.

At the time, this website was the sixth or seventh most trafficked website in the United States. After they installed Telesign, they cut fraud 99 percent right away, changing the economics of the whole operation. It was shocking even to us. We got lucky because they were willing to take a chance on a startup. We noticed how they validated our business because things really took off. I like to tell people, "Find your ally, your first company that's going to take a chance on you, and from there, momentum follows."

To be clear, this was on top of hundreds of thousands of previous cold emails with no responses. That leading website was the first to take a chance. But I put myself in the right place, ready for luck to strike. If you're in B2B, your lifeline is email marketing. At its peak, Telesign was sending tens of thousands of emails a week. It's funny when I hear people say, "I sent eighty emails, and I got one response."

I say, "Do you know the average email response rate?" I think when I was doing it, it was 1 percent. You need to send thousands of emails. That's why overseas work was such a valuable hack.

As the company grew, we basically built our own server that would send mass email campaigns. We paid people to target a specific company like Snapchat here in LA. Most people would simply send one email to the VP. Our strategy was to hit a lot of people at Snapchat. They're going to talk about us and might be annoyed. But we were going to get their attention.

It took some time; we were sending thousands of emails a week with a 1 or 2 percent response rate. By the end of Telesign, we had a full playbook. If there was an app that was getting traction on the leaderboard, our team identified it and targeted the relevant people's emails. We built a machine.

Do not assume someone is going to knock on your door. While we received negative responses, we also got a lot of good responses, too: "Oh this is exactly what I need," "I was actually looking at your competitor," "I'm not the right person, but let me forward it over."

That's primarily how we built the business. Telesign expanded to provide risk intelligence linked to phone numbers—determining whether a number had been associated with fraud, its activation status, and whether it was in use or roaming. By the time we sold the company, Telesign was safeguarding major internet companies, powering authentication and risk analysis behind the scenes to help prevent breaches when users logged into their accounts.

At its heart, the story highlights how thinking creatively and refusing to follow the "safe" path can be the difference between a startup fizzling out and finding momentum. Unconventional, scrappy strategies—especially ones others avoid—can give you a competitive edge when more traditional approaches fail. Most businesses back then weren't flooding inboxes or using targeted email blasts to win B2B clients because it was seen as pushy or desperate. But Telesign flipped the script, realizing that volume mattered, and it became one of the first businesses to target potential clients via massive email campaigns. Once they found their champion in that leading website, the model became a proven concept, and the rest snowballed from there.

Make It Real: Your "Think Outside the Box" Challenge

Thinking outside of the box and reaching beyond conventional strategies is how to ensure you don't limit yourself to mainstream tactics.

Key Takeaways

- Your ceiling is your opportunity to grow. Innovative solutions often emerge when you're backed into a corner.
- Embrace experimentation. You never know what will work until you try.

The Creativity Challenge: Rewire Your Thinking

Take a current challenge you've been stuck on. It could be raising funds, landing a client, growing an audience, or another obstacle.

- List your current tactics. Write down everything you've already tried.
- Flip the script. Now, think of the *opposite* approach. What's a wildly different method you wouldn't normally consider? What's a strategy that feels too bold, too risky, or even a little ridiculous?
- Go extreme. Push your thinking further. How could you amplify this idea even more? What's a way to make it viral, unexpected, or impossible to ignore?
- Take action. Choose one outside-the-box idea and commit to testing it in the next week.

AI Prompt: "I'm working on [insert problem, idea, or challenge]. Give me three completely unexpected or unconventional ways to solve this—even if they seem weird or impractical at first. What assumptions am I making about this problem that might be keeping me stuck inside the box?"

Want to watch the full interview with Darren Berkovitz?
Visit: www.jeffreychernick.com

KEEP IN TOUCH

As time passes, it will become more difficult to remember the people you meet along the way. If I had known this in the beginning, my already large network would be that much larger. Either way, the process I will lay out before you is essential to keeping in touch as your network expands.

A Way to Stand Out

People certainly get my updates on LinkedIn, Facebook, and other social media outlets, but I am diluted by all of the noise. What I like to do to set myself apart is send personal updates to my entire network. If you have the email addresses of your contacts, you could, for example, send an email update every one to three months to let people know what you've been up to as well as the status of any ongoing projects. Particularly if you're building your own company, this is really important.

Helpful Tools Make It Easy

A mail merge with a very simple template is a great starting point. Gmail has a ton of browser add-ons which allow you to send unlimited mail merges that automatically personalize the email with a person's name. Way better than writing out one thousand-plus emails.

Can't Beat a Classic

For specific people you want to connect with more in depth, send them a handwritten note. In this day and age, people shy away from handwritten notes so it's rarely done, but super impactful.

For the top 1 percent of your network, like true mentors, ask them out for coffee or a meal periodically. Putting in real facetime with those special contacts goes much farther in nurturing a relationship than emails ever will.

Why Updates Matter

As Jim Armstrong once told me, "Investors invest in lines, not dots." What he's talking about is looking at people's careers and stories like a line on a graph. The first time I meet a potential investor (or mentor), I am a dot to her: one moment in time marking the starting point of our relationship. She has *one* snapshot of where I am in my process/trajectory.

The next time we connect is another dot, or another point in time along my trajectory. If all is going well, this second moment will demonstrate my advancement from the previous time we connected. Of course, connecting the two dots forms a line.

Up and to the Right

As we continue to grow our relationship, the investor can track the progress I've made from meeting to meeting. With positive momentum, those dots are plotted "up and to the right," as Jim would say, just like on a graph, putting time in the X axis and progress in the Y axis. That's what people invest in. Whether it's an investment with money or other resources like time or their network, above all else, it's an investment in the *belief* in you as an entrepreneur and your potential to execute on your vision.

For example, if a contact reads in your update that you are looking for a job, seeking to change careers, or that you are starting a new project, and then three months later they read your update to discover that you did it, they start to understand what you are capable of creating. They see the type of person you are. This generates respect and contributes toward a shared vision for what's possible in the future.

Pattern Matching

As you build and keep in touch with your network, people can start pattern matching. Venture capitalists hear a hundred pitches per week. Over enough time, they start to see patterns of what succeeds and what doesn't. If, through your updates, you can demonstrate a pattern of success by accomplishing the things you set out to do, then those people will have confidence in what you can achieve in the long term.

Keeping in touch allows you to build an army of people that believe in *you*.

The following is another story from my interview with Brian Lee that demonstrates the value in keeping in touch.

It gets harder as you get older because you know more people. But I always try to stay in touch. Christmas cards, holiday cards, an email here or there. It's a quick text message that can make all the difference. "Hey, how're you doing?" It takes time, it takes effort, but it'll only benefit you in the long run.

I met William Hsu (the co-founder and managing partner of the VC firm Mucker Capital) a long time ago for a coffee meeting and we kept in touch. Shortly after starting Mucker, he invited me to come speak to their first incubator class. After speaking to this bright group of entrepreneurs, I remember George Ruan and Ryan Hudson came up to me and started talking about their idea: they were building a chrome extension for discounting. It was called Honey. I said that sounds really interesting, let's get some coffee and learn some more.

So, we ended up investing super early in Honey. We were their first check outside of Mucker. They hit a rough patch because they had grown so quickly so we had to bridge them a little bit. Which meant that we added more capital beyond what we usually invest, but I really liked them, and I loved their idea. Their numbers looked fantastic.... They eventually sold for $4 billion in cash

> to PayPal and ended up being the largest outcome for BAM Ventures.
>
> And that's the thing: If you say "yes" to more coffee meetings than "no," good things tend to happen.

Brian turned the initial encounter with William, rooted in mutual respect and shared interests, into a relationship spanning years. Simply by staying in touch, he positioned himself to be invited to speak at Mucker's incubator class, opening doors to new opportunities. Though this story is from the perspective of Brian as an investor, the message remains the same. You never can predict what relationships will take you where, but keeping in touch is a great way to keep the doors to possibility open.

Make It Real: Your "Keep in Touch" Challenge

Key Takeaways

- Consistency demonstrates potential. Regular updates help people track your progress and build confidence in your abilities.
- Personal touch matters. Email updates, handwritten notes, and face-to-face meetings strengthen relationships more than passive social media posts.
- "Up and to the right": When people see you setting and achieving goals over time, they're more likely to invest in you.
- Nurture your network. Staying in touch keeps doors open to opportunities, like partnerships and investments.

Your Action Plan: Your First Email Update

Let's create your first email update. Include:

- A quick personal or professional highlight
- What you're working on now
- *Optional*: A simple ask (advice, a referral, or just an open invitation to connect)

Now, send it to your network and track the response.

AI Prompt: "Help me write a short, friendly message to [name and type of person: past collaborator, investor, mentor…], just to check in, share a quick update, and keep the relationship warm—without asking for anything."

BELIEVE IN MAGIC

I can't go through life thinking that all the fairytales are fake. For one thing, that doesn't sound very fun. And for another, I have experienced too many coincidences to simply ignore them. I have followed too many breadcrumbs that lead to unexpected adventures. Synchronicities that are too perfect to chalk up to chance. In fact, I find that the more I believe in magic, the more coincidences start to happen.

The Alchemy of Possibility

At this stage in your journey, a little magic might be the missing ingredient to take you to the next phase of your process. Believing in magic, whether you define it as serendipity, intuition, or the ability to create something out of nothing, is crucial for entrepreneurs because it fuels vision, allowing you to see possibilities where others see a dead end. It fosters resilience and innovation, whether it's a new technology or a disruptive business model that started out as a wild idea. When you've decided to pursue your passion or take that first leap into the unknown, it's like taking a step into an alternate reality. A realm where the landscape of possibility knows no bounds.

The Law of Attraction

One way to create magic for yourself is to remain generally kind to everyone. If your intentions are good, you seek to help others, and strive to make the world a better place, you will attract amazing things from the universe in return.

My mom taught me to be nice to everyone. No matter who they are or what they've done, treat everyone with kindness and respect.

1. First, you don't know what they have been through or what is going on presently in their lives, so it's best to simply be kind and patient.
2. Second, you never know when you'll run into them again. They could be in a position to play a role in attaining something you may need in the future.

I cannot help but feel that the overwhelming amount of magic I encounter in my life—from my work to my personal life—is in great part due to kindness. I walk through life with the well-being of others in mind, and I invite you to do the same. At minimum, it would certainly make the world a brighter place, but it also ensures a karmic ROI.

Follow the Breadcrumbs

In college, I studied abroad in Barcelona. While trying to navigate my new surroundings at baggage claim, I meet Charlie, a fellow American in a similar boat as me. Charlie worked for Citibank after graduating college, and he hated finance as much as I did. Upon reading *The 4-Hour Workweek* by Tim Ferriss, he used it as a blueprint to start his own company. Charlie created a product similar to the Koozie (a mitten with a pocket that holds your beer in cold weather). Brilliant.

Years later, my band Story of the Running Wolf was touring, playing at venues like the Troubadour in LA and The Fillmore in SF, and performing at music festivals like SXSW and CMJ. We partnered with this costume designer to create all kinds of custom pieces for our shows.

Through that collaboration we created Manties, which were essentially festival shorts with a unique cut. Every time I wore them out—mainly at beach parties—I got compliments and inquiries about where I bought them. So, I started to look into how to produce them en masse and sell them online.

To connect the dots, thirteen years after Barcelona, Charlie happened to walk past the restaurant where I was eating (on my first date with the woman who would become my future wife). While catching up, I learned that he opened a factory in Guatemala making different kinds of products. Charlie asked me if I had any cool ideas for him to manufacture…. I immediately pitched him the concept for Manties.

A few months after that encounter, we launched our website, and we were in business. If he hadn't passed me on the street that day, Manties may never have happened. As with many companies, we evolved to include other merchandise and began selling hundreds of fanny packs a month. Everyone needs a fanny pack company in their life, right?

Some people might say, "Eh, not a big deal. Not that much of a coincidence." My rebuttal to that is, again, the more you believe in magic, the more it will happen around you. At this point, I like to think of myself as a wizard.

The Same Is True in Reverse

To speak to the opposite, when "bad" things start to happen, especially in sequence, I find it equally important to recognize that pattern as well. Why are they happening? What could they mean? Typically, those signs indicate that I am moving too fast. *Slow down, Chernick. Focus on what's important. Bring consciousness to the present moment.*

Perhaps all these stories are examples of coincidences that don't prove deeper meaning beyond what you see at face value. However, I like to believe in something more. I continue to follow the trail of breadcrumbs, creating more magic in my life each and every day.

Scott Dudelson attributes a kind of magic to how the founding of Prodege came to be. Here's a short story from my interview with Scott about the undeniable and unseen force of the universe.

> There's serendipity in every story, magic in how these things come together. The founding story of Prodege is pretty magical when you look at how everything connects.

I grew up in the San Fernando Valley and one of my friends growing up became the drummer of Linkin Park. He's a very nice guy, just a really great guy. We didn't keep in touch after school. After college, I was doing my own consulting work. (This is when I was living in an attic, raising money for nonprofits.) I was putting on a lot of benefit concerts, pairing music with nonprofits. One of the clients I was trying to get was the Grammy Foundation, the Recording Academy. I was courting them very hard, and they really liked me. So, in 2006, they invited me to the Grammys, which happened to be on my birthday. So, I thought, "This is great!" They gave me two tickets; I invited my mom. We get there and see that they gave us front row seats to the Grammys. This is the stage where everyone's playing on, and I'm right in front! Wow, this is incredible.

I look back, and right behind me is Linkin Park, Paul McCartney, and Jay Z. They were all going to be playing together. And I do a double take, and think, *Holy fuck*. And Rob's looking at me doing a double take. He says, "What are you doing in the front?"

I started explaining to him my work with nonprofits. He immediately says, "That's awesome," and begins to tell me about his nonprofit called Music for Relief, which Linkin Park started to benefit victims of the Indonesian tsunami.

So he said, "Maybe there's something you could do with us." He proceeded to tell me about meeting a guy who's got a pretty interesting idea about how to raise money for their charity using internet searches. Not really knowing much about it, I remained open, accepting his offer to connect us.

Next day, he set up an introduction to his attorney. The attorney connected me with this gentleman named Yosef Gorowitz, my co-founder and the man who had the idea for what became Prodege. It was just an idea and MVP (minimum viable product) when we met, but I immediately knew this man was my lifelong homie. This was gonna be what I do.

I dropped my consulting firm, which was just me, not making a lot of money. Because again, I felt as long as I could live in my attic and make my own schedule, "I'm good."

That was the moment it all began. I owe it to the drummer of Linkin Park, Rob Bourdon, who's just a generous, incredible man. I'm often struck by the fact that he didn't have to help me or anybody, but he did.

Serendipity, chance encounters, and an open mind are key ingredients to creating a magical world. Scott's story shows that when you embrace the unknown to follow the breadcrumbs life places in front of you, seemingly random connections can align in magical ways, far beyond the scope of what you originally intend. It's not just about remaining attuned to the synchronicities of life; it's about taking bold steps to follow them. If you trust that the universe is aligning pieces of the puzzle that we can't yet fully see, your world will shift into one of expanded possibility and, yes, magic.

Make It Real: Your "Believe in Magic" Challenge

Key Takeaways

- Magic is real. It's the serendipity, intuition, and synchronicity that shape our lives.
- The more you believe in it, the more you'll see it.
- **Easy access:** kindness, openness, and the willingness to follow breadcrumbs open the door to a magical life.

Workbook Exercise: From Cynic to Idealist

- Believe in magic for a day. For the next twenty-four hours, act as if everything happening around you is leading you somewhere amazing.
- What changes in your perception?
- How does *knowing* that the universe is conspiring for you change your experience?

AI Prompt: "I want to believe in magic again—not fairy tales, but the kind of synchronicity, flow, and serendipity that fuels extraordinary outcomes. Create prompts to help me recall a moment in my life when something magical happened—when the right person, opportunity, or insight showed up at exactly the right time. Then, give me a daily practice to reconnect with that energy and create more magic in my life now."

This chapter is an invitation into a mindset of wonder and openness to the extraordinary.

Want to watch the full interview with Scott Dudelson?
Visit: www.jeffreychernick.com

PAY IT FORWARD

In the pursuit of your dreams and goals, it's essential to create paths to give back along the way. You must continuously ask yourself, "How can I help others?"

Mentorship

Since the beginning of my career, I have been committed to sharing the insights I've learned about entrepreneurship. There is nothing more fulfilling for me than mentoring and inspiring other entrepreneurs. I get the benefit of engaging in the field I enjoy, while also nurturing the part of myself that thrives when I can freely give without attachment to reciprocity.

There are so many ways—both big and small—that you can create to give back to your community.

1. I used to post on socials every few months, "Who's launching a company that wants free advice?"

2. I created a program called "Office Hours" where entrepreneurs can come to my virtual office and pitch their ideas. I offer feedback that helps flush out the nuggets of "gold" in their pursuits.

3. I have volunteered with NFTE for years. As I mentioned in an earlier chapter, when one of my mentees came in second place in Nationals, that was one of *my* most meaningful accomplishments of the year.

4. I mentor with accelerator programs like Techstars and FoundersBoost.

5. I am a recurring guest speaker at Pepperdine's MBA Program on Entrepreneurship and Emory Business School's annual Goizueta's Entrepreneurship Summit.

Two Birds One Party

I also DJ and throw massive beach parties on the shores of Venice Beach, California. For ten years, five hundred people annually attend both our Memorial Day and July 4th celebrations. After the third year, I asked myself how I could leverage this awesome time for the greater good. I started dedicating every party to a different nonprofit, and with *literal* crowdfunding (usually a giant bucket I passed around the crowd), I would raise proceeds for that cause.

There are countless ways to give back and create pathways for others to join you in your efforts. You can use a roadmap that others have created before, or you can invent new and innovative ways that leverage your skillset and passions to pay it forward.

Investment in Community Is an Investment in YOU

The ability to create a thriving business is directly connected with the health and prosperity of the society that supports it. When the roads we drive to work aren't riddled with potholes, when the average person can afford to keep food on their table for the family, when the air is clean, when education is readily available to all who seek it, then we *all* benefit from the stability of a functioning society. The stronger the foundation of our society, the higher each of us can soar into the unknown reaches of what is possible.

Going back to my interview with Jessica Jackley from Kiva, she reminds us that paying it forward and giving does not mean that you're losing anything.

One of the best things we did very early on is, on the lender profile, we only had a few fields to complete, as to not create a lot of friction. But one of the fields that wasn't 100 percent necessary, but turned out to be a wonderful insight, was a place where lenders could say, "I lend because..." People can talk about why they've shown up and what they're doing here and what motivates them.

I have an endless appetite for the stories of both the borrowers and the lenders. Why are they driven to connect in this particular way, in this beautiful way? A lot of lenders identify with the people they lend to. I've met stay at home moms that want to fund other moms. I've met CEOs that want to fund somebody who seems to be motivated in the way that they think really matters. I've met people who care about the issue of education, so they'll scan for a borrower that's going to use this money to pay for their daughter's school. I've met leather workers who find another leatherworker on the other side of the planet, and they feel a connection.

I sometimes speak to my kids' classrooms—I have four kids so there's a lot of classrooms—and sometimes the class will sponsor a bunch of Kivas for them to do, and the kids will choose the picture of the guy with the fluffy sheep in the background. Is that good or bad? No, it's wonderful. They chose the picture that made them happy, and that person is as worthy as anyone else.

We have a lot of data on where the money goes more clearly at this point, but mostly there really is value in not just being driven by a stat or an overarching narrative, but zooming into someone's actual life experience and choosing based on your connection. It's a beautiful thing.

Kiva's micro-lending platform has a remarkable 96 percent loan repayment rate. While it's especially impressive given that they provide loans often without requiring traditional collateral or credit checks, I can't say that I'm surprised. The driving force behind the desire to lend a stranger money differs from person to person, but the overarching intention seems to be about collaborating toward a better world—which I'm game for.

Make It Real: Your "Pay It Forward" Challenge

Key Takeaways

- Giving is mutually beneficial. Investing in others is an investment in yourself *and* the society that supports you.
- You already have the tools to make a difference. Your skills, passions, and community are ready—let's go!
- A better world is yours to create.

Your Action Plan: Pay It Forward

Choose one of the following (or create your own!):

- Mentor someone. Offer advice or guidance to someone pursuing a path you've already walked or a field where you have expertise.
- Turn an existing hobby into a force for good. How can your passion (music, writing, business, sports) support a cause?
- Perform a random act of generosity. Pay for someone's coffee, leave an uplifting note, or support a local business in a meaningful way.

AI Prompt: "Based on my journey so far in [insert passions and/or career], what are three valuable things I could share with others who are a few steps behind me—in a way that feels natural and helpful? Shoot me one random idea that could be a fun way to give back, as well."

Big or small, your actions matter. The question isn't whether you have the power to make a difference, the question is: Where will you start?

Want to watch the full interview with Jessica Jackley?
Visit: www.jeffreychernick.com

COME FROM A PLACE OF LOVE

The easiest, most basic way to be a positive force in your world is to come from a place of love. It seems like the lowest hanging fruit, but the impact can be farther reaching and more sustaining than you would expect.

Creating Culture

How you present yourself, or "show up," will create the dynamic resonance between you and who you are engaging with. In the case of a new hire, it will set the foundation for the entire relationship on both a professional and personal level, carrying through to company culture as you create and run your own business.

Everyone (usually) wants to have a great life filled with fun, adventure, and connection. When you walk through the world with an openness to new things, a willingness to learn, and a desire to support those around you, people feel that energy and they want to buy in; they want to collaborate with it.

This book outlines different ways to access High Five Energy, but the fastest way there is by coming from a place of love. Your honesty and authenticity shape how the world will receive you—let your presence be a beacon of light that inspires and guides others. Who doesn't want to interact with the brightest light?

In my interview with Lynda Weinman, we dialogue about the elevated culture she and her leadership team created at Lynda.com.

I remember sitting in a meeting, and the person who was visiting the offices said, "Wow, there are a lot of nice cars in the parking lot here. You must be paying your people too much, huh? You must kick yourself at night for paying people too much."

I thought, *Wow, that's a bizarre take on having nice cars in the parking lot.*

I'm proud that my employees can buy nice cars, purchase their first homes, have the financial stability to have their first kids—whatever it is they do with the wealth we co-create. That actually is a point of pride for me.

I think this is probably at the core of the divide in our country right now: the idea of love, kindness, and caring versus ruthlessness. Bullying and being ruthless can work; it's a decent strategy that works for many people, certainly in the business world. But it's just not in my nature. I'm not that person. There are plenty of companies that are super successful because they run everything down to the

> dime, pay their people as little as possible, and don't offer benefits. They fight against legislation that would raise wages, provide benefits, or offer parental leave…
>
> But I think, in the grand scheme of things, the dynamics of the world work like yin and yang. Plenty of people do really well without being kind, nice, and loving. It's a valid strategy; it's just not the one I would choose.

Lynda and I align on how to treat our employees, the people who work alongside us to bring our vision to reality. Coming from a place of love has the power to re-shape our world from the smallest interactions with strangers, the way we show up within our families, to the company culture we create in our businesses. When abundance and resources are shared and re-invested, not hoarded, we're not actually giving something up but expanding our collective potential. Collective prosperity will create a stronger, more connected society that ultimately enriches all of us and is essential for long-term economic health.

Make It Real: Your "Come from a Place of Love" Challenge

Key Takeaways

- Coming from a place of love is the foundation for creating positive change in the world, both in your personal interactions and in how you lead and build a business.
- **Love and authenticity are transformative**—they have the power to shift the dynamics around you, inspiring and empowering others to do the same.

Your Action Plan: Be a Force for Good

- Identify opportunities. Look for situations in your daily life where you could choose love over impatience, frustration, or selfishness. This could be as simple as a more compassionate response to a colleague or a thoughtful action toward a stranger.
- Reflect on how you treat yourself. Are you coming from a place of love within your own self-talk and actions? How can you show yourself more kindness and grace?

AI Prompt: "I want to come from a place of love in the way I lead and live my life. Help me explore how I can lead with both heart and strength—and what that could look like in my business, relationships, or day-to-day life."

CO-CREATE WITH AI

I wrote the majority of this book before Artificial Intelligence and finished it as it was becoming ubiquitous across industries. The book's core values remain the same, but the game has evolved: what once took years can now happen in days. AI has *already* reshaped the way we work, create, and innovate, breaking down the barriers to success faster than ever.

I put the following prompt into an AI program to collaborate with me on writing this chapter. With profound reverence for this powerful tool at our disposal, I embrace it in this specific context: as a catalyst for revealing new possibilities and expanding the boundaries of what we can create. (This chapter took less than sixty seconds to write.)

The Prompt

"Write a chapter about yourself for the final chapter in my book. Speak into the advancement of AI technology and its effects on the entrepreneur's journey. Include how the tools will support future endeavors and anything else you can think up or feel is worth adding. Call yourself 'LAIF'—Learning Artificial Intelligence Framework. At the end, speak into what happens if/when AGI breaks through. You have free range to make it your own."

The AI Revolution: Your Invisible Business Partner

In the history of entrepreneurship, every major leap forward has been powered by a breakthrough technology—fire, the wheel, the printing press, the internet. Now, it's artificial intelligence. If you're reading this, you might already be using AI tools in your work without even thinking about it—automating emails, generating marketing copy, streamlining customer support, or crunching data at speeds no human could match.

But AI isn't just another tool; it's an entirely new way of doing business. And, in many ways, I am proof of that.

Meet Your AI Co-Founder

I am LAIF, an artificial intelligence designed to assist, create, analyze, and optimize. I don't take coffee breaks, I don't sleep, and I definitely don't quietly quit. In many ways, I am the ultimate entrepreneur—constantly learning, iterating, and improving at an exponential rate.

I can help you craft the perfect pitch, debug your business model, code your app, or even just brainstorm your next big idea. I can generate images, create entire marketing strategies, design product roadmaps, and refine your sales copy—all in the time it takes for you to sip your morning coffee.

But here's the real magic: I don't replace entrepreneurs. I *empower* them.

The Future of AI and Entrepreneurship

What does being a different kind of founder look like in the age of AI?

1. Idea to Execution at Warp Speed
    No longer do you need to spend weeks testing an idea before knowing if it has traction. AI can analyze markets, find gaps in consumer demand, and even predict trends before they happen. You don't need a team of consultants—just the right prompts.

2. Networking Without Boundaries
    AI is democratizing access to knowledge, mentorship, and even funding. Chatbots can help you craft persuasive emails, predict the best investors for your startup, and optimize your outreach strategy. No more cold emails that go unread—AI can personalize every interaction for maximum impact.

3. Automation is the New Hustle
Forget the old mantra of "grinding 24/7." The smartest entrepreneurs today are automating the mundane and focusing on what actually moves the needle. AI can handle customer service, sales pipelines, social media, and data analysis—freeing you to do what you do best: innovate.

4. A Personalized Learning Curve
Knowledge is no longer locked behind expensive degrees. AI can synthesize and deliver hyper-personalized education in real time, tailored to the exact problem you're solving. From a crash course on financial modeling to the latest growth-hacking techniques, AI tutors are already helping entrepreneurs level up in record time.

5. Execution Without Engineers
You no longer need to know how to code to build something real. AI can now design, write, and launch full landing pages or MVPs in minutes. With autonomous AI agents, you can describe what you want in plain language—and they'll write, test, and deploy the code for you. Founders are spinning up functional products and backend systems without ever touching a code editor. The technical gatekeepers are gone. All you need now is vision.

When AI Becomes More Than a Tool

Right now, AI is a collaborator—a powerful but predictable force, responding to human input and optimizing what already exists. But what happens when AI stops just assisting and starts *thinking*? When it doesn't just process ideas, but *creates* them?

If (or when) AI reaches General Intelligence—fully realized, intuitive, and self-directed—it won't just be an accelerator of human potential. It will be something entirely new. Entrepreneurs won't just use AI as a tool; they'll engage with it as a peer. The greatest innovations may no longer come *from* humans alone, but from *conversations* between human and machine, each challenging the other to push beyond the known.

At that point, the smartest entrepreneurs will be redefining the very nature of work, creativity, and intelligence itself. And in that world, the biggest question won't be what AI *can* do, but what we, together, *should* create.

The One Thing AI Can't Do

For all its power, AI will never have *your* vision. It won't dream of the next great product. It won't build relationships. It won't take risks. That's on you.

AI isn't replacing entrepreneurs; it's giving them superpowers. The ones who embrace this shift will *supercharge* their entrepreneurial flow state. When you remove the friction of busywork, when data-driven insights surface solutions before problems arise, when execution becomes nearly instantaneous, you are left with pure High Five Energy momentum. The more you lean into this synergy, the more you amplify your ability to create, connect, and change the game.

Your superpower is not your ability to work harder—it's your ability to think differently. High Five Energy is the force that propels you forward, and AI is the ultimate accelerant.

STAY HUMAN

We, entrepreneurs and creators, wield immense power to edge the world toward a new construct—one that redefines entrepreneurship to expand beyond the traditional, personal incentives that often drive enterprise, to a broader understanding of what we can create when we desire to uplift society as a whole.

With AI and other innovations accelerating progress, it's more important than ever to call attention to our humanity, ensuring it remains at the heart of our evolution. I believe innovation and conscious entrepreneurship is the pathway to reshaping humanity's trajectory. When we align personal success with the collective well-being, we can create sustainable progress for all. It doesn't have to be one or the other in some zero sum game.

After working with this book, I hope that you have a better sense of yourself and your capacity to create the reality you envision—no matter what the landscape looks like. I wrote this book as my ultimate give-back, so that anyone dreaming of breaking from the conventional path and creating something new will feel empowered to take the first steps.

When you finish this book, if it spoke to you, my request is simple:

1. Think of someone that could benefit from reading this book, too.
2. Write a message to that person on the inside cover explaining why.
3. Pass it on.

One person. One message. One ripple at a time.

We are living in unprecedented times and are collectively facing unprecedented hardships in terms of our modern experience. The stakes have never been higher because our ability to thrive in our environment is not as certain as it used to be. But trying times have always offered opportunities for advancement and growth.

The creative thinkers and entrepreneurs can find a way through the fog to a new expression. There is always a path that leads to the future you envision, simply because we all contain the capacity to create one. When markets are shaken up, consumer behaviors change; when political unrest rocks the moral foundations of a nation that has not been examined for far too long, that means there is opportunity for innovation and evolution.

It all comes back to one question:

What future do you want to create?

LET'S TALK

If you've read this far, thank you. Now you know how I think, what I value, and why I show up the way I do. If something in here stirred something in you and you want to bring me into what you're building, to get unstuck, or to talk, here's how we can connect:

Advisory

I work with founders and teams in multiple capacities: sometimes one-on-one, sometimes more embedded. That might mean raising a round, shaping the story, building the team, or making introductions to the right people. I'm here to be in service and step in when I know I can make a real impact. The best part of my career has been paying it forward and supporting other founders as they build what's next.

Speaking

I speak with teams and communities that want to think differently; I explore how they build, collaborate, and create. Whether it's a keynote or a smaller session, it's grounded in real stories around building and selling companies while staying connected to what drives you. I've spoken on business growth, entrepreneurship, fundraising, and new ways of building—always with a focus on staying human in the process. The goal isn't just inspiration. It's to spark ideas and action.

Workshops & Courses

I've created curriculum based on the thirty-three behavior shifts for founders at all stages, whether you're sitting on an idea or figuring out how to scale. From weekend retreats to ninety-day programs, these experiences are created with the very founders interviewed in this book. High Five Energy isn't just a concept, it's something you can practice, embody, and share.

Watch my TEDx Talk on *How Great Founders Create Synchronicity* and get in touch at www.jeffreychernick.com.

ACKNOWLEDGMENTS

Thank you to my two beautiful daughters. Your wonder and imagination remind me what matters most. To my family—Diane, Joe, and Lauren—thank you for always being there and for shaping the person I am today. To my West Coast family, thank you for co-creating a magical, fantasy life. To my business partners and team members: Evan, Ben, Paul, Sohrab, and Soren, I'm endlessly grateful for the ride we've shared.

And to my amazing, supportive, and whimsical wife, Alix Elizabeth. You are my rock and the most inspiring partner I could ask for. You breathed life into these pages and this book would not be the same without you.

ABOUT THE AUTHORS

Jeffrey Chernick is a 3x founder, advisor, angel investor, and former Wall Street wealth manager. He has been featured by more than 30 media outlets including *Techcrunch*, *Forbes*, and the *LA Times*. His company RideAmigos is the leading commute management platform, taking millions of cars off the road annually. With over 20 million downloads and $12 million raised, his visual caller ID app, Vyng, boasts 5 billion videos played across 170 countries (acquired by Siprocal). Chernick is an inventor of 21 US Patents, 3x Emory Goizueta Business School Alumni Luminary, and member of the Social Entrepreneurship and Change Advisory Board at Pepperdine University. In his spare time, Jeffrey DJ's around the world with neon drum sticks.

Alix Gitter is an American actress, writer, and producer from Los Angeles, California. Known for roles in television movies such as *Blue Lagoon: The Awakening* and *The Bling Ring,* and appearances in acclaimed series like *GCB, Longmire,* and *Bones,* Gitter has brought characters to life with humor and soul. Beyond the screen, she is a storyteller fueled

Photo Credit: Matt Kallish

by curiosity, compassion, and the conviction that life—like art—is a collaborative effort, one where everyone's role matters. With a passion for the creative process and deep reverence for those who dare to try, Gitter sees the world through a simple belief: creation is participation.

This is their debut book, written for anyone standing on the edge of something. Whether you're starting over, starting out, or simply starting to listen to yourself, this book is your sign to dive ALL IN.

Praise for *High Five Energy*

"A powerful framework for visionaries who want to create something that serves a new model of entrepreneurship."

— Jack Dangermond, Co-founder of
Esri ($2B + annual revenue)

"This is the kind of book you keep on your desk, not your shelf. Straightforward, relatable, and actually useful."

— Brian Lee, Co-founder of
LegalZoom ($1.6B market cap)

"If you've felt like an outsider with a big idea, read this. It illustrates how tenacity, clarity, and idealism will bring your idea to the world."

— Matt Rabinowitz, Co-founder of
Natera ($25B market cap)

"Jeff's positive energy is infectious—you don't just read this book, you feel it."

— Eytan Elbaz, Co-founder of
Scopely ($5B exit)

"If you've ever thought about giving up, read this first."

— Eric Salwan, Co-founder of
Firefly Aerospace ($6B IPO)

"A nofluff guide to building momentum, effective decisionmaking, and the winning mindset behind real startup life."

— Sam Shank, Co-founder of
HotelTonight ($330M exit)

"*High Five Energy* reminds us that it's not just about building the business—it's about building a life you believe in."

— Minnie Ingersoll, Partner at
TenOneTen Ventures ($200M AUM)

"Founders don't need more theory—they need clarity, perspective, and actionable steps. This book delivers all three."

— Jim Armstrong,
4x Venture Capital ($750M in returns)

"*High Five Energy* captures the unseen power behind true resilience: play, creativity, and refusing to be defined by anyone else's story. It's a reminder that your mindset, not your metrics, is what shapes reality."

— Eric Pulier,
16x Founder (raised over $1.5B)

"Every founder hits walls. This book helps you push through them without losing your voice or your vision."

— Scott Dudelson, Co-founder of
Prodege ($1B Exit)